The YES Life

I've had the privilege of having front-row seats in Tes Jahnig's life. And in every season, I've watched her choose the YES LIFE yet again. I've watched her dig deep, find faith for the moment, and jump in with both feet and open hands. Many will want the 'YES LIFE' that God offers – few will actually choose it. I'm grateful she did because my world is better for it. No doubt, as you dive into the pages of this book – your life will be too.

– Dylan Jahnig, Husband and Senior Pastor Linc Church SA

* * *

Our yes is paramount to our life's trajectory. Tes has framed this poignant key, sharing her heart with honesty, humility, and beautiful articulation. The empathetic tone of this book builds a bridge over assumption and connects Tes's journey to our own. The heart that is burning through these pages comes and runs with me in the fullness of the Father's intent – no more captivity, no more limitation. It's expansive on the other side of our YES.

– Nat Taylor, Speaker and Prophetic leader

* * *

Well thought through and fresh out of the heart, Tes takes the reader on a vulnerable trip into her own soul. Putting things in a fresh perspective, she makes us fall in love with the Creator, helps us be honest with ourselves, and then shows us the hope of saying YES. I love every word of it. It's pure, honest, and deep.

– Marcel and Cody Gaasenbeeck, Redemption Church Netherlands

* * *

Writing about what you think is so different to writing about what you have lived out. I have had the benefit of experiencing many years of Tes' leadership and friendship. Her words carry significant weight, no frills or exaggeration, just the truth of her pursuit of Jesus. I have watched her choose calling over comfort on many occasions and have personally, with many others, lived as a beneficiary of her costly 'YES'. So, very simply – this is a book you want to read.

– Mark and Cath Slevin, Campus Pastors Linc Church Hilton

* * *

Tes opened my heart with her words. The vulnerability and easy style of her writing contain a powerful vision of a life hidden in just one word – YES. This book is full of hope for a better way. It is full of practical wisdom to unlock an impactful, meaningful life. Her words resonated within me, and I began asking the following questions: What have I missed by simply not saying 'YES' to God? What *can* happen if I just say 'YES'? Tes shows us that opportunities will abound if we just embrace YES. Thank you for 'The YES Life' – it is simple, thought-full, incisive and profound.

– Andy Clark, Lead Pastor Urban Life Church

* * *

My friend: You have given us a handbook for the mountain top, the valley, and the ordinary in-between moments of life. I invite all readers to join you in the YES life. It is an honour to grow with you as you ask questions every believer should ask. I look forward to the person I will become after implementing the tools you have given us. The YES Life is relevant and necessary and I am so glad to be living in the time of Tes Jahnig. I'll keep saying YES.

– Nande Boss, Writer and Preacher

***

I remember the first time I had the privilege of meeting Tes. I immediately thought that she should write a book and that it would impact many. Tes is an insightful and wise thinker, and she is a dedicated follower of Jesus who has continued to say YES to following Him wholeheartedly. I am certain that the fruit of her YES and the commitment to His call, no matter how challenging it has been, will be seen for all of eternity.
– **Lucinda Dooley, Global Lead Pastor Hillsong Church**

***

This book is not only a beautiful reflection of your authenticity and skill with words, but also of wisdom and the powerful redemptive rhythm to be experienced by all who are willing to hurl their whole selves into this Christian life.

Your ability to articulate how the Holy Spirit has gently moved you from a place of fear into a formidable faith – into a YES life – is a brilliant testimony of what Jesus does with a surrendered life. Thank you for your YES, and may every reader be challenged to take a step towards the freedom and fullness offered to a life fully yielded to the King.
– **Brittany Jones, Passion City Church Atlanta**

***

'For this reason I kneel before the Father, from whom every family in heaven and on earth derives its name. I pray that out of his glorious riches he may strengthen you with power through his Spirit in your inner being, so that Christ may dwell in your hearts through faith. And I pray that you, being rooted and established in love, may have power, together with all the

Lord's holy people, to grasp how wide and long and high and deep is the love of Christ, and to know this love that surpasses knowledge – that you may be filled to the measure of all the fullness of God. **Now to him who is able to do immeasurably more than all we ask or imagine, according to his power that is at work within us, to him be glory in the church and in Christ Jesus throughout all generations, for ever and ever! Amen.'**
Ephesians 3

This prayer from Ephesians has been prayed over you many times since we met you and Dyl, dear Tes. When we read the first chapters of your book, we can only marvel at our great God. Your understanding and the beautiful revelation of our God of BIG YES is a testament to Christ dwelling in your heart and how you have rooted yourself in His love, and now that is being displayed through the powerful words you have so beautifully written in these chapters. May that revelation be imparted to the many who read and ponder your words, and may they, too, find the depths of this love from our lavish and amazing Father. We write these few words with a full, grateful and delighted heart, dear Tes. We are very privileged to share in your radiant journey as you boldly profess our Father's dealings in your life through the messy and marvellous moments, the tiring and tremendous times, and the small no and BIG YES revelations.

– Melanie Dyer – 3Ci Church

* * *

Tes, I think you're awesome, and I can't wait to see the domino effect this book 'The YES Life' will have on the men and women exposed to it directly and indirectly. May the 'Yes Effect' ripple into the world and down the corridors of time.

– Jaci Mungavin – Lead Pastor Anthem Church

The YES Life | Tes Jahnig

MOVING BRAVELY FORWARD

Published by Yes!Press
(Yes!Press is an imprint of Quickfox Publishing)
Cape Town, South Africa
www.quickfox.co.za | info@quickfox.co.za

First edition 2024

The YES Life: Moving Bravely Forward

ISBN print: 978-0-7961-9080-2

Copyright © 2024 Tes Jahnig

All rights reserved

No part of this publication may be reproduced, stored in a retrieval system, or transmitted, in any form or by any means, without the prior written permission of the author:
amber@lincchurch.com

Editor: Catherine Jenkin & Amber Mac Millan
Cover design & image: Ashleigh Duggan

Follow the author on social media:
Facebook: @tesjahnig / @thelincsisterhood
Instagram: @tesjahnig / @thelincsisterhood

To my One and Only Jesus, my first love and best friend.
This book is my first fruit, so, therefore, it is Yours.
Thank you for saying YES to me.

'As God is faithful, our message to you is not "Yes and no." For the Son of God, Jesus Christ, whom we proclaimed among you – Silvanus, Timothy, and I – did not become "Yes and no." On the contrary, in him, it is always "Yes." For every one of God's promises is "Yes" in him. Therefore, through him, we also say "Amen" to the glory of God.'
2 Corinthians 1:18-20 ESV

The YES Life is Dedicated To

My Dad
The hilarious truth is that he would have favoured the audio version because I think he thought me too wordy. Despite not being here on Earth, I know deep within that he sees the words through the thin veil of Heaven, and I can feel his pride. He championed every big 'deal' I pursued. I will never forget the day he smiled as I told him, 'I think I've written a book, Dad.' He always knew I could do this. This first one is a thank you to him. Thank you for your open lap, big heart, and even bigger smile. I promise I'll record the audio.

My Dyl
Dylan, you are the one who, more often than not, tips my YES over the edge. Your zealous pursuit of my fullest potential is why I have stepped into more opportunities and favour than I could have found on my own. This is my story, but in essence, it is ours. It is my most profound privilege to live every YES with you.

My Kenz, Tae-tae, Honny and Joel
You have cheered me on and dreamed with me. You've encouraged me to keep going even though you don't fully understand what that means. You have sat on my lap as I typed and brought tissues as my story found pages. You have formed and shaped my YES more than you could ever imagine. Thank you.

My people

Thank you to everyone who has spoken this book into being. You have believed in me, risen far above my self-doubt, and brought me courage when I question my ability. Thank you for being an integral part of every YES I have said.

Table of Contents

	Introduction 1	
1	A Big YES and a Small No 3	
2	When No Becomes YES 11	
3	The Greatest YES 17	
4	The YES Life Starts with a Choice 23	
5	The YES Word 31	
6	When Ordinary People Say YES 41	
	A Note 49	
	A Prayer for the Yes Waiting before You 50	
7	YES to God 51	
8	YES to Marriage 57	
9	YES to Children 65	
10	YES to Church 75	
11	YES to Leadership 81	
12	YES to Women 87	
13	YES to Pain 97	
14	YES to Gratitude 109	

15	YES to Giving It All Away	121
16	YES in the Middle of the Night	127
17	Do it Afraid	135
18	Words Matter	145
19	What is the YES Life?	151
20	The Key Principles of the YES Life	159
21	An everyday YES Life	163
22	No is a Full Sentence	169
23	The YES Effect	173
24	It's Still YES	183
	Conclusion: This is Just the Beginning	191
	Thank You	193
	Connect with Tes	197
	Back Cover Copy	195
	Endnotes	195

Introduction

'One of the few things I know about writing is this: spend it all, shoot it, play it, lose it, right away, every time. Do not hoard what seems good for a later place in the book, or for another book; give it, give it all, give it now.' – Annie Dillard[1]

One may assume that a 'first book' would be a humble start. In every way, mine is. The YES Life is gloriously naked in its vulnerability and humility. As you open this book, you may assume that I would have kept some back for another book and another time. I think I have. As I grow in life, there will always be more to come.

We start every book we read with assumptions. I put my hand up and claim this. I am at the top of the list of people who may assume. I assumed so much about 'The Book I Would Finally Finish.' I thought and deliberated for so long, and there was a time when I truly believed these words would never leave my digital archive because I hoarded these words for the perfect year, the ideal place, and the perfect time.

Life is short, and it is harrowing in its brevity. As cognisance of this becomes conscious knowledge, we are left with a choice. Will we live? Will I live holding nothing of myself back from the world? Will I live sharing the depths of my God and the transparency of my person? Will I take a risk on the riskiest part of life: me?

This book is my significant risk. The risk to truly live. The imperfectly lived out YES Life. I have said YES many times. Some have paid off. Some have not. Some have fuelled me forward. Some have not. Saying YES has cost me so much of myself. This book has been a strenuous personal exercise. It has asked me to bear my soul and surrender my heart to what I truly believe and value. It has challenged my beliefs. It has caused me to question my motivations. It has forced me to heal. It has allowed me to grow. It has given me the greatest gift, even when no published piece of paper was in sight. It has given me a bird's eye view and a window ajar into the depths of what is me. For this, I will be eternally grateful.

I pray you'll read about my reckoning and embrace yours, too.
That you'll say no and goodbye to find the YES within your heart.
You'll stop at nothing to know the greatest YES said for you.
I said YES to life in the hope you will, too.

Welcome to the YES Life.

1 | A Big YES and a Small No

In the Beginning

It was a perfect place. ALL OF IT. Each day was an adventure, living and walking. Working the gift that was this paradise garden. Walks in the cool of the day, having intimate conversations with the One who formed his flesh. Man alive, vital and free. He could lead, create and define things, name, and order existence. Then, without any effort, he woke up complete and whole because he had a woman by his side. A being so exquisite and different but no less valuable. Finally, he had someone. An answer to his aloneness. A solution to his solitude. She was mysterious and wonderful to enjoy and share breath with. She was 'it'; together, they were a rare and profound image of the One they walked with. She was exactly what he needed to live completely; he was her name-giver. They were together. Naked, perfect and without shame. They only knew this way, and it was good. Together, they were good.

Explore, adventure, create and identify, he tells them. Be curious and confident in your newfound home. Use what has been given to you and multiply it. This is the opportunity given to them. The garden is spacious and roomy. It is perfect because He made it. Complete because they're in it. It's a playground of epic proportions. It beckons their involvement and presence. They have permission to build something vibrant and shape communities. And in all of that, YES, we find one small no. A wise command from a loving Father: to avoid something that would separate their connection. They had free and abundant access to everything except just one little tree.

A big YES and a small no defined their world. YES to all they could see, taste, and touch, except for the one tree. The Creator and friend asked them to stay away from it because of its power to devastate them, leading them to abandonment and death.

Many of us know how this creative poem ends. The deceiver, the thief, questions the Creator's intent. He manipulates the man and woman and sows a seed of doubt into their trusting hearts. For the first time, they can't see His goodness. The serpent challenges their access to everything they have by focusing on the one small thing they are told to stay away from. They disobey their God – with consequences they never dreamed of. The enemy distorts the YES and no of God right in the beginning, and humanity would never be the same again.

If we read the beautiful Creation poem from within our limited humanity, we will miss the essence of the story. I know I initially did.

This is so much more than a picture of God creating and man failing. This is the first moment we see God's true intent and heart.

This is where it all begins, and we bear witness to a God, a Father who would stop at nothing to win His children back and reconcile us to Himself once and for all, a God with a master plan and divine strategy. All because, in the beginning, they missed the invitation to the YES Life and instead just saw the no.

1 | A BIG YES AND A SMALL NO

The gift of this story is that we can look in and see what happened in the beginning and decipher what that means for you and me. We can get to know the Creator, our Heavenly Father, who gives us a big YES and a small no.

I first encountered this idea of 'God of a big YES and small no' when our friend and Pastor, Rory Dyer, shared his thoughts about the essence of the Genesis story in 2011. It changed my life. People throw the term 'life change' around flippantly, but this was a defining moment for me. I won't forget it because it shifted the trajectory of what I believe and know of God. It is the foundation and inspiration from which this book flows.

What we believe of God directs and informs our behaviour. Seeing God holding a BIG YES in His hands has shaped how I view life. It has formed how I read scripture and understand the Bible's narrative. It has altered the way I interact with people. It has pushed me to new levels of intimacy and growth within my marriage. It has affected the way I parent my children. It has caused me to go after what I was born for.

It was the moment when the lights turned on.

As a young girl growing in a relationship with God, I made unhelpful assumptions about who He is. Those assumptions were based on what I experienced through my encounters with people. I'm sure, if you are honest with yourself, you may say the same. I spent so much time allowing my environment and people to shape what I believed about God. Instead, I should have sought the truth from the Source Himself. When I looked around, what I saw seemed limited and restricted. Through words and behaviour, it felt like people said 'no', and I assimilated this all as 'there is not enough; you are not enough.' In my immaturity, I let my circumstances shape who God was. I shrank God to a form that I could comprehend. I tried to fit Him into my story instead of allowing Him to shape mine.

I missed some of the foundational and fundamental parts of His character – THE BIGNESS of His YES, how He exists outside of time and space, and that there is so much room for everyone and everything in Him. He is a God of purpose, passion, growth, wrestling, calling, anointing, gifting, opportunity, and access.

He is a YES God for a YES Life.

'He was supreme in the beginning and – leading the resurrection parade – He is supreme in the end. From beginning to end, He's there, towering far above everything, everyone. So spacious is He, so expansive, that everything of God finds its proper place in him without crowding. Not only that, but all the broken and dislocated pieces of the universe – people and things, animals and atoms – get properly fixed and fit together in vibrant harmonies, all because of His death, His blood that poured down from the cross.' – Colossians 1: 18-20 MSG

It happens without us even knowing it, over time, throughout our life experiences. We paint a picture, in our minds, of who God *should indeed* be. He is who we think He is in our finite minds. For many of us, He is full of laws and regulations. Headmaster and judge. A God who holds people at a distance. A God who asks us to work our way

1 | A BIG YES AND A SMALL NO

towards His heart. A God who punishes sinful behaviour and restricts us when we don't get it right? A big no-God, perhaps?

But I've learnt that placing who God is within the boxes of our curated existence is dangerous.

It feels incredulous to me to write this now. At one point, I truly believed that God *was* the reason for the lack in my life. He was the author, so He must be the problem. I felt that God made my existence and opportunities smaller. I convinced myself that God's YES was not for me.

Have you ever felt like you're living in a perpetual state of lack? There is just never enough. Everyone seems more 'blessed' and better off than you are. It's frustrating, isn't it? I was in this place of questioning and comparison for many years. I knew there must be more, but I had yet to access the fullness of freedom and joy God offers us all. Hearing those words 'God of a big YES' for the first time, it felt like my soul woke up. I connected wholeheartedly with this simple statement. The concept spurred me to discover the extent of God's YES and what it meant to respond to the invitation of the YES Life given to all.

My response to my circumstances shifted when I encountered this new message. A message that resonated in the depths of who I am. For deep does indeed cry out to deep, and as this happened, I began to believe that the YES Life is for me. As I journeyed forward, I saw this YES in the consistency of what I read within Scripture. A message that showcased who God was from the beginning – a God of a big YES and a small no. The bigness of His Heart and the magnitude of His Grace shone through the pages as the weight of YES and no shifted within my belief system.

It began as I looked at God differently. I realised that God was not my limitation. I was my own and most significant limiting factor. And I wrestled with this ever-evolving question: Could I have it all? A calling, a passion, family, significance, purpose, and influence. What if they could all coexist? What if all of it was possible with Him, the God of a Big YES?

God's YES is wide and open. In Christ, opportunity always outweighs opposition. Alongside His wide, available YES is his protective and safe no. His no ensures His children are secure within the boundaries of grace and mercy. We don't see any other answers of no, but one. Why? Because God knew what was good for them. The tree of knowledge was mighty, and it held within it more than they could carry or consume. It would open their eyes to all the things that would corrupt them. It would lead them towards circumstances that would cause them pain. It would give them what they thought they lacked but, in essence, would keep them from the One they loved most. They would have to wrestle and grapple with what they believed. Sin, shame, and death would have access to their hearts. The small no was for their ultimate benefit. It was for our benefit, too. God knew then, and He still knows today.

I believe that every boundary has a blessing attached to it. Even when we see the small no, we experience the bigness of the YES. The YES is always significantly more prominent for those who embrace the invitation of the YES Life.

1 | A BIG YES AND A SMALL NO

I'd love to tell you that everything shifted overnight and that, somehow, this discovery allowed me to live content and fulfilled for all my days. That didn't happen. The journey from here was indeed forward. It was, however, slow.

I didn't immediately say YES to the invitation I saw of this YES Life. I was scared. Unsure and torn between what seemed natural and what felt like a pull of God. My mind was taking time to catch up to what my heart inherently knew was true. It was the road less travelled that I was embarking on. There was no map, and I did not know what awaited on the other side. I was fearful. I was doubting myself and God. I was questioning what I had heard because I felt inadequate and insecure. I knew God was calling me to figure out something that would change my life and possibly the lives of many more. Maybe even yours? And I wasn't sure I had enough to say YES to make this YES Life journey something all people could see, understand, and take hold of.

Let me take you back to a moment that defined me and caused me to sit up and look at my life marked by no. This was the moment that began the journey to YES.

2 | When No Becomes YES

How did I get here, and why was I nervously hiding behind a projector screen? My heart convinced me that I was somehow invisible, blind to everyone who 'should' care and unnoticed by those I was so desperate to be accepted by. My constant attempts to be everything to everyone led me towards a downward spiral of 'never enough.' and brought me to a place of deep loneliness.

Someone had said something that, yet again, stabbed at my insecurities, and in an attempt to protect myself, I hid. I took my pregnant self and sleeping baby and snuck behind the old-school projector screen as the congregation hung out after the service. I could hear the fading chatter, and it seemed no one missed me; no one noticed my absence, and even my husband left thinking I had gone home without him. He phoned me a few minutes after locking up and leaving and soon realised I was alone in the building with our child.

This bizarre yet heartbreaking moment shaped me. It marked the beginning of my journey out of hiding. Although oblivious to the implications still to follow, the lights had 'turned on', and a new chapter was emerging as I stepped out from behind that screen.

Until this point in my life, I had waded around in an ocean of uncertainty. I was still determining who I was and what I stood for. I was fragile, quickly rattled, and full of deep-seated insecurity. My heart ached for freedom from the weight of people's thoughts and opinions and freedom from myself and my limiting beliefs. The problem was that I needed to figure out what to do. I was uncertain. I felt unsafe in the community and spaces I was a part of, and in a desperate attempt to cope, I lowered my expectations to the level of my circumstances instead of lifting my eyes to the level of His truth.

As a 23-year-old mother and wife to a passionate Imagineer, I found myself planting a church before I had time to understand what that meant. This unknown adventure excited and exhilarated me. I wanted to be the all-in-one champion wife and mother. I wanted to be the go-getter communicator, worship leader, writer and Pastor. I desperately wanted to 'give back' to Jesus everything He had given me. However, my need to serve and repay His kindness was out of balance and misinformed. In reality, I was just so immature and so newly saved. Somewhat blissfully naive but also alive with my young faith. I was hesitant, not yet brave enough to filter what others would say. I was caught in a web of pleasing people and determined not to disappoint those I loved and the ones I thought I needed to impress.

I had no idea how to let my YES be YES and my no be no. I was the buffer between the 'needs' of the well-meaning congregation and Dylan's leadership. Week after week, I was on the receiving end of oblivious unkindness. Knowingly or not, people treated me like the 'Pastor's wife', a new and confusing term I had not encountered before. Whether or not they did it intentionally, I was manipulated because of my vulnerability, and this moment in my life wounded me deeply.

I see how resolute defiance in me grew as I hid behind that screen. I felt caught off guard and out of control. It hurt, like my soul was aching. Human beings do crazy things when they are pushed into a corner. We go to extreme lengths to protect ourselves. I did the only thing that made sense. I vowed to keep myself safe from people, even those I loved most. I decided that no would be my stance. It would dictate and define my behaviour and my responses. I would not say YES to anything where I could not control the outcome. If there were even a possibility of pain, I'd walk away. At this point, it seemed like the YES Life wasn't meant for me.

No would mean a less exciting life, but it would be predictable. I said no to my husband. I said no to church. I said no to people. Ultimately, I said a big, loud no to God. I built a fortress around my heart. A fierce, resilient wall that would no longer allow me to get hurt. I stepped out of conversations. I abdicated leadership responsibilities. I refused to show up. I put down my guitar, and I stopped singing.

And then, to my dismay, I started to die on the inside, little by little. Every. Single. Day.

My aversion to YES kept me in a holding pattern longer than I should have allowed. I held myself back from becoming who God created me to be. I held myself back from pursuing meaningful relationships with people who wanted God's best for me. I sat in a space that withheld me from the YES Life I dreamt of living. The kind of life that saw me leading and living on the edge of my seat in anticipation of what God would do next. The type of life that saw me at the forefront of championing a God-breathed life in all people.

The kind of life I knew I was born for.

I shut myself off to YES and, in turn, to God. I closed myself off to possibility and adventure. I stopped taking risks and settled for a safe life. When I first encountered the reality of Jesus, I determined that I would live uninhibited for God. I'd take hold of His undeserved grace and take bold risks as a thanks offering for my rescue, and yet, here I was, bound up in my defiant no. Fuelled by unforgiveness and bitterness, I let go of my desire to live a wild, holy life marked by passionate obedience. The YES Life.

But I was unhappy.

Over time, years, and through the intentional kindness and friendship of people and ultimately by the grace of God, I didn't stay in this place of resistance. I slowly opened up my tight fists, clinging to the vow I made behind that screen, and slowly relinquished the power that no held over me.

As humans, we make these irrational and erratic inner vows when we are under pressure and stress. We fight, or we freeze. For all of us, the need to self-protect is genuine and natural. When we make quiet promises like these to ourselves, however, we give them too much power. We may find some certainty for a while, but over time, they cause us to become stagnant, stationary, and unhappy.

We were never designed to stand still or stay wounded, and the good news is that God can break through our walls. He is much greater than our sorrow and pain. God is more potent than our stubborn inner promises of no. He is more robust than we could ever imagine. He is more passionate about us living our best lives. He is kind. I am so grateful He fought for my heart and never gave up on the YES I truly wanted to say.

He, friends, is the One who took my ordinary self, my hardened heart, and began to chip away at my no. Using the pain, I didn't want to feel or face, my weaknesses and the insecurities that drove me to this point in the first place, He led me to the end of myself so that I would, without a doubt, be able to say YES to Him again. He convinced me of my position as a daughter first. He convicted me of my eternal forgiveness and the grace that flowed through my heart and soul. He stripped shame from my life and especially from my past. Little by little, and layer by layer, I began to breathe again. Hope again. Trust again. Live again. Eventually, I said YES again.

3 | The Greatest YES

For the first time, I could see God's big YES, and I felt like something inside of me was being awakened, like an ember finding its flame.

A fire inside me had rekindled and was burning with this new realisation. The narrative over my existence was YES and not no. A big YES God allowed me to dream more than I ever had. I felt free to imagine the possibilities without the fear and shame of not achieving the outcome. I knew that life would never be the same again. Still, the nagging question lingered: What now? What exactly did this big YES mean for my everyday life?

This began my daily steady walk within the YES Life. Through this walk, God shaped and transformed my existence, little by little. Day by day. He began to manoeuvre and mould my thinking around YES and the responses that followed. Looking back, I can see the gentle yet swift way He moved me towards the YES Life I longed to live.

Embracing the big YES of God changed many things, but the best change it brought about was how I now read the scriptures with fresh eyes. I no longer saw it as a means to an end. Instead, I saw it as a beautifully interwoven, connected story. I saw it as a journey of seeing God restore humanity to Himself by saying one small, powerful little word: YES. A God who would fashion and shape history to showcase His YES, which embodies His generosity towards us from age to age.

I stopped seeing the rules and limitations, and instead, I began to see the opportunities and invitations from His heart. How his generous character burst through time, meeting His people over and over again.

As I lost myself in the poetry and Bible stories, I discovered the significance of all that was lost at the fall of humanity in Genesis. I had always been so focused on the fall of man. Now, all I could see was the big YES and the divine plan of redemption that followed. I began to see how a strategic plan was promised and delivered within the Old Testament. A plan that shouted YES to the people. The promises of God echoed through Abraham, Isaac, Jacob, Esther, David, Gideon, and Isaiah. The divine act of One who would come to restore and re-establish God's big YES of all time.

The Old Testament, bursting with YES promises, ends almost abruptly. The prophet Malachi once more calls the people of Israel to turn again towards their God. And then, no one speaks.

Nothing.
Absolutely nothing.

The Heavens are silent. For hundreds of years, no prophets or priestly voices have been recorded. Then, out of nowhere, a baby is born. Matthew begins to recount this miracle that rocked the world. It was a birth so otherworldly that rulers sacrificed baby boys, shepherds went on long journeys to visit Him, and Eastern wise men followed a supernatural star to bring Him gifts. With one infant's cry, the Heavens open again. God speaks, and His great YES unfolds.

His name is Jesus.

Jesus, fulfilling the Old Testament laws and promises, is the ultimate picture of God saying YES. He is the greatest invitation to the YES Life. Every blessing, prophetic promise, command, and calling given to humanity over time culminates in a YES because of Him.

Jesus shows us one Earth-shattering thing: He is the true and most excellent picture of God's YES to me, to you, and to all of us.

Jesus. His Earthly life, bold death, and supernatural resurrection are the resounding declarations of YES over my life. And yours.

YES to freedom.
YES to mercy.
YES to righteousness.
YES to healing.
YES to wholeness.
YES to redemption.
YES to love.
YES to change.
YES to life.
YES to fruitfulness.
YES to hope.
YES to grace.

When you read The Bible as a story of love and redemption, threaded together by grace, you begin to see the fullness of the Father's heart. It is not God who says no to Adam and Eve. Instead, it is Adam and Eve who say no to God. God has always said YES. Even his no is a pause for a better YES to come.

What a thought. To suddenly know and see the sheer extravagance of this YES-saying God. He said YES first. His YES is the greatest YES of all time.

Have you ever stopped to think about Jesus as a human? A young man. Flesh and bones, sitting in a garden, pondering His death alone. Give yourself a moment to think about Him.

I've been to Gethsemane in Israel. I've sat where they believe Jesus retreated to pray when the others were too tired to do so. I watched the gentle breeze create an ebb and flow between the olive tree leaves. I've felt the deafening silence of being alone in that garden.

I pictured a man facing what he was about to face. Jesus would have seen the temple, the courts, and the city's gates in this garden. As the fullness of God in human form, he would have had supernatural insight into the betrayal that would disappoint Him. The torture, hatred, and death. Sitting in this humble garden, I imagined his excruciating struggle towards YES. His honest and intimate conversation with His Father. A pleading for some other way, yet, in all the torment, He lands on *'YES, GOD – not my will but your will be done.'* (Luke 22:42)

I'll do this for them, Jesus decides. All of them. I'll say YES for them because my YES will become theirs, too.

I imagine Him saying, *'I see my daughter, Tes. Young and unsure. I see her heart. I see her life circumstances. I say YES. I'll do it when she can't look at herself without feeling self-loathing. I'll do it when she begrudges her age and stage with small children at home. I'll say YES for the times she resented her husband's freedom in a season of young motherhood. I'll do it for the moments when she wants to quit. I'll do it for the moments when she doubts what God has placed within her. I'll do it when she questions my heart and my ways. I'll do it for the times when she desperately wishes her life would count for something more.*

I'll do it for all of them. I'll do it for those who have yet to discover Heaven's depth and breadth. I'll do it for those with little idea of who they are and the potential that lies within. I'll do it for their freedom. I'll do it for their wholeness, healing, and future. I'll do it for them to come alive in the big YES so that things will never be the same for future generations. I will say YES so that, one day, they can say it too.'

Jesus said YES first, from a place of perfect love. He said YES to death so that you and I can say YES to life in return.

It seems unbelievable to think that I thought I was the one who made the grand gesture of moving towards God and saying YES first. My YES was not the one that made me who I am today. My YES was the small response to the greatest YES of all time: Jesus Christ. He died and rose again, conquering sin and shame and removing the sting of death. Jesus reunited us with our Father forever.

I don't know much, but I know this: His YES called forth mine. His YES beckoned me home toward His heart and perfect plans for my life. My YES was a human response by faith to align my head, heart, flesh, and spirit with the divinely predestined life God had in store for me – the YES Life.

4 | The YES Life Starts with a Choice

'In the end, that was the choice I made, and it doesn't matter how hard it was to make it. It matters that I did.' – Cassandra Cassidy, *City of Glass.*[2]

Knowing that God went before me, that He made the first move and chose me long before I chose Him, speaks volumes about His Heart. How intentional He is so that we can be free. He created us with the liberty to choose Him and His ways. We are not robots who live by engineered default settings. We are genuinely free.

This drew me to God many years ago and continues to draw me to Him today. It's what makes Him the best Father – the kind of Father we all know we need, right? A Father who lovingly and without control gives us a powerful gift: the ability to choose.

The fact that we have choices sets us apart from every other created being. We do not live by primal instinct as animals do. Instead, we can think and use our human reasoning to make choices every day. This is what makes us powerful. We are not slaves to one way. We have options.

Contrary to what people may think and speak of this Christian life, followers of Jesus are free beings. We can create and curate the existence we aspire to and dream of. We hold immense power to shape the trajectory of our lives. We do this by making everyday choices that lead us towards our destiny.

THE YES LIFE

Viktor Frankl, a neuroscientist and survivor of the Holocaust, wrote a harrowing yet hopeful account of his experiences during his time in a concentration camp. In 'Man's Search For Meaning,' he says:

'Between the stimulus and the response, there is a space. In that space is our power to choose our response. In our response lies our true freedom. For everything can be taken from a man but one thing: the last of the human freedoms – to choose one's attitude in any given set of circumstances, to choose one's way.' [3]

He was held captive in one of the most cruel, dark places known to our world, Auschwitz. Yet, somehow, he concludes that even when we feel like there is no way out, we are powerful because we still have the power to *choose*.

The greatest lie we are told is that we don't have options and that we're stuck in our circumstances. This lie ultimately says God has limited us to a small life because of His restricting ways. But nothing could be further from the truth. We are an empowered people, and we can choose how we respond to what is in front of us every day. That is the essence of what it is to be a human being who lives with meaning.

My early days of motherhood felt long and arduous. *'How could I achieve anything beyond survival when I was pregnant with a toddler attached to my hip?'* I was painstakingly slow. I had *always* been fast, but now, I wasn't. Looking back, I was so young, and in my mind, far too young to be a wife and mother at twenty-three. I lived many days feeling like I was fresh out of options. The world around me seemed to be racing forward, and I was going nowhere. I was circling my own season and felt like the world was leaving me far behind. Like my real life had closed in on my future and my dreams.

My husband was pioneering and pursuing his heart to build a church like we hadn't seen before. I desperately wanted to join him, but money was tight, and we had these tiny babes, so it made sense for me to stay home. This meant I spent most days at home reading first-word picture books and doing peg puzzles over and over again.

I did everything within my human ability to try and repurpose my longing for more into this early stage of motherhood, but the nagging in my heart to do something 'great' *within motherhood* would not go away. I lived with this relentless and burning desire for my life to count as a woman, but it felt as though the monotony of my season was taunting me as I changed nappies and rocked babies, day in and day out. I knew that raising children was *the* most important thing I would ever do, but I couldn't see past the mundanity of it all. I felt invisible. Many days, I wondered if God had forgotten me.

There was no way around it: I feared simultaneously missing out and making mistakes. If I said YES to motherhood, I would say no to everything else, right? I was painfully unsure. I saw myself being left further and further behind, so I made fewer choices. I was indeed stuck.

The lies in my mind and my limited view grounded me in that season. The longer the days felt, the more frustrated I became. I was so trapped in my 'either or' narrative that I convinced myself *this* church story was not for me. I told myself the story that a healthy family and church could not co-exist, and in doing so, I convinced myself that church would be Dylan's thing. At the same time, I pursued something else: a personal training and fitness career alongside motherhood.

The more broken I became, the harder I trained until I was forced to face the consequences that my hiding in something else was having on my marriage and children. After nearly 18 months of running away and immersing myself in something I could control, I gave up my mission to build my own life for the sake of a future with my husband and two small children.

This was a defining moment. In hindsight, I can see how it established so much of my YES when I laid myself down to walk into a story bigger than me.

Everything starts with a choice. We are free to say YES or no to each opportunity.

Where we find ourselves today is directly related to our choices; we will become the decisions we make daily.

Saying YES is only possible when we realise there is always a choice. The YES Life is a choice. We are not stuck in our life circumstances. We have access to options, even when it feels like there are none. Choosing the YES Life means seeing the possibilities, seeking them out, and weighing them up. Choosing the YES Life means looking for opportunities to say YES.

My story took a significant turn towards something new when I chose to say YES to a life where everything I dreamt of could co-exist.

Marriage, motherhood, church, leading and creating. A life where I can make choices, in freedom, around my roles and contribution to this world daily.

Andy Stanley says: *'Our direction, not intention, determines our destination.'*

We can have the best intentions in the world, but the truth always lies in this simple idea: our direction leads us to our destination, not our intention. As I get older and life gets fuller, I learn how crucial it is to be strategic and intentional with my daily decisions. Each seemingly small decision, each YES or no, will lead me somewhere.

We don't drift towards good decisions; we prioritise them. We do not land in a YES Life by default; we must choose it. We put ourselves where YES is possible and decide to live this way. Saying the best YES – in any shape or form – starts from a place of making an active choice.

I chose to face the Tes, who fiercely resisted and stubbornly pursued her own plans. I chose to search my heart in the early stages of motherhood. I chose to desire more and be comfortable with that choice. I chose to come out stronger.

This significant YES opened my heart to a grander vision. It enabled me to live, lead, and work with my husband *as a mother* rather than running from a role I had been entrusted to. One that I was born for.

I chose to turn my heart toward God's divine plan, and what followed were more decisions that have led me to where I am now.

But this didn't just happen. I had to lean into the discomfort of laying things down. Being 'both and' – motherhood and ministry – one calling upon another – isn't always easy, but it can be both. Both can fit into the story. 'Both' is my story.

I said one initial, wholehearted YES to a life that looked different from what I thought it would – a 'both' kind of life. I chose YES then, and I still choose it now. The reality of these big and small decisions has produced a gloriously messy, big life – my YES Life.

Making decisions begins with conscious thinking and then lands in action. The action then leads us towards the trajectory we need to follow to realise the dreams and desires that God places in our hearts. He so beautifully gives us uncluttered views of what could be. He sets within us a burning conviction and zealous passion. He allows us to lie awake at night, wrestling towards the preferred future we long for. He beckons us towards destiny and hopes we will say YES to it all.

I decided my life would be marked by a resounding YES and an even bigger AMEN – a 'so be it' to God – even when it doesn't make sense. When faced with opportunities to step up and into things that I know align with God's heart, my bias would be towards YES, despite the inconvenience, risk, or cost.

I yearn to see what lies on the other side of audacious YES decisions. I live to do the things God asks of me without hesitation. I'm curious and intrigued by what happens when I choose to partner with God.

Often, the junction of YES sits in my gut. This otherworldly knowing where my YES must land. Am I always right? I don't think so. Like one preacher once said, 'We're only ever 50% sure.' I have learnt, however, to trust the whisper of the Holy Spirit. The gentle wind words that blow through my heart. The impression of what sits right. I have come to recognise when the YES keeps my mind moving. The YES Life is inextricably linked to your inner voice, and your relationship with God. It is deeply spiritual.

What choices are you making? Every day, we make choices that define our lives.

'How do you want to live your life? How do you want to play the game? Do you want to play in the big leagues or the little leagues, in the majors or the minors? Are you going to play big or play small? It's your choice.' – T. Harv Eker

God places an open door before us. He is the God of the big YES. His invitation to all of us is to walk through this open door and into His presence, a bold YES to the YES He said first, a YES to faith and working out the details later. We choose not to walk through with all the answers and the perfect scripted ending. Instead, we walk into and towards YES, trusting He will lead us into a promising future.

I chose YES because I didn't want to live an ordinary life. A safe life looks good on paper, but I want more. I want to live a life marked by beauty and adventure, no matter what.

YES is a decision we first make when no one is watching – in the secret place, when the lights are out, without anyone cheering us on. YES is said when we don't know the reward or accolade on the horizon. YES, choices come from our hearts as we obey God's direction, even when we don't have the complete picture. We say YES because we know our YES unlocks the grander vision.

What I've found to be most beneficial is choosing the YES way before I even get there. YES exists beyond my superficial feelings. Many years ago, I decided that YES would be my preferred posture. Even if unsure, I would lean towards YES anyway. When I didn't have all the answers, I would say YES. At the end of it all, I want to know I lived a bold life. I want to keep moving bravely forward.

In these early moments of my journey with God, I knew He would not leave me in my world defined by no, but little did I know that the road towards YES can be marked with great pain, and there is so much to surrender along the way.

5 | The YES Word

YES.

Three letters that hold potency, force, energy and weight.

A word that can mould and shape the present. A word that can unfold and unravel the past. A word that can catalyse and define the future for generations to come.

YES.

YES is a catalyst.
YES is a response.
YES is a conduit.
YES is more.
YES is infinite.
YES is unlimited.
YES is opportunistic.
YES is optimistic.
YES is ready.
YES is big and bold.
YES is risky.
YES is a stance.
YES is a belief system.
YES is a posture.

YES is a power word.

To try to understand YES, I began to look for people in the Bible who had said YES despite significant opposition, uncertainty, and at great cost. What if I could learn to lean into the immediate YES that I know the world around me desperately needed? What if I could learn the art of quick-footed radical obedience in an age where no one wants to do what they are told? What if I could harness the power of saying YES to the right things and step into the fullness of life God was inviting me into?

I've come to know and believe that obedience is still a thing.

I've spent the last few years following the pandemic vacillating between what I am and what I am not 'allowed' to do. The lines were blurry as we all discovered our different needs and strategies to cope and overcome. With that coping and negotiating of what is 'okay' and 'what is not' has come a questioning of the importance of obedience. I have landed on the thought that obedience still matters.

'Samuel replied: *"What is more pleasing to the* LORD: *your burnt offerings and sacrifices or your obedience to his voice? Listen! Obedience is better than sacrifice…"'* – 1 Samuel 15:22 NLT

The prophet Samuel has come to speak to King Saul, who has disobeyed God by following his preferences and ideas. He had a habit of doing this. God gives specific instructions, but he ignores God and does his own thing. Because of this, he is soon to be stripped of his title as king. In this bold statement above, Samuel tells Saul that his disobedience demands a sacrifice. If he obeyed God, sacrifices would not be needed to make things right.

When obedience goes first, the need to atone falls away. In Jesus' life, as the greatest demonstration of obedience, we see the ultimate sacrifice, which removes the need for ours.

Am I saying that obedience does not require any sacrifice? Not at all. Obedience will always cost us something – that's part of the point. We lay down our will for the will of another. Obedience will, however, never remove us from the safety of our destiny and secure eternity that is ours in Christ Jesus.

Did you know that our generation is the first to prioritise self-interest over community well-being? Generations before us lived for community first, but we have chosen to live a life full of self. We are not a people who like to put ourselves in positions of self-sacrifice and surrender. When I first heard our generation being defined this way, I knew I wanted to live differently, in a higher way. A life where obedience goes before me and paves the way for the life I am destined to live. The YES Life is founded upon obedience and faith. The YES Life revolves around something and Someone greater than myself. The YES Life presents the opportunity for us to live beyond the realm of self and ask: *'What truly is best for the community?'* This provoked my journey of studying those before me who chose YES despite themselves.

My exploration of scripture landed in the story of Abraham. It gripped my heart and set me on the pathway to discovering much that I needed to learn about obedience. Abraham said YES again, and again, and again.

To understand Abraham's story, we need to track his journey from Haran to Canaan. In Genesis 12, it seems a man enters out of nowhere. The walls of Babylon have fallen, and humanity is in chaos again. People are dispersed and wondering. They are confused, isolated, and uncertain. Does this sound familiar?

God begins formulating and constructing a strategic rescue plan within this disorder. A nation will rise from chaos, and the Messiah will be born.

He chooses an unknown man, an unlikely character named Abram, to set the wheels in motion. We're given this picture in scripture of a voice from above calling this ordinary man, with a promise of more, towards a holy adventure. He's asked to leave his familiar. To go and establish himself and his family somewhere new and unlikely. Abram is promised that his YES to leaving will release a mighty inheritance, a great nation. From him, an expansive group of people would come, and he would be blessed beyond his human comprehension. It would take one thing – just one word: YES.

We're told *Abram went*.

The Bible doesn't give us the context we need to acknowledge the power of Abram's obedience. In studying his life, we gather that he lived in the Ur of the Chaldeans. It was a superpower nation in its day:

the largest city in the world and the epicentre for trading within the Mediterranean. It was a place where his father had established himself and his family. Ur was on the way to Canaan.

Abram's father fell short of Canaan as he became enamoured with the culture and the opportunity to build his empire. Abram's family was rich. He was wealthy because they'd set up a home within an economic hub. Abram had influence in Ur. He had history and currency and held power there. However, when God asked him to go, he packed up and made the journey to Canaan almost immediately.

What is Canaan? Where is Canaan? All God said was that He would show him this place. He failed to mention that Canaan was uncultured, rough, and uncivilised, unlike Ur. No one in their right mind who lived in Ur would consciously choose Canaan. And yet, when God asks Abram to leave and go to Canaan, he does so immediately.

The YES to Canaan is less about the place than we realise. God asked Abram to leave an old way, habits, and identity. He was leaving behind his name. In exchange, he would have to embrace something new – a new way, pattern, and identity. Saying goodbye to Ur meant saying goodbye to Abram. Saying YES to Canaan meant opening the new door of destiny – a door to his new name and identity, Abraham, the Father of many nations.

God is the God of Hello and Goodbye. This is the essence of the YES Life. We say goodbye to something out of obedience and hello to all that YES holds by faith and with great expectation.

THE YES LIFE

Abram heard 'Go' and said 'YES', unlike his father, who settled. Abram uprooted his family and followed God's lead. That was all God needed: a willing and obedient heart, a tenacious and YES-oriented spirit, and someone hungry for the YES Life. God isn't seeking our perfection – He's just seeking our obedience.

A divine 'Go' is presented to all of us in our lifetime. Often more than just once. It is up to all of us to choose to leave something before we're willing to go somewhere new.

Abram, renamed Abraham, would say an even greater YES in the future that changes history for you and me.

In Genesis 22, much has happened since the simple 'Abram went' statement. He's grown impatient in his desire for an heir to give birth to this mighty nation and a great inheritance. In desperation, his wife, Sarah, has convinced him to produce a son with his slave, Hagar. This complicates everything, and the illegitimate heir, Ishmael, is cast out into the desert.

After many years of waiting and silence, Abraham and Sarah miraculously bear a son, Isaac. They're old, it's a miracle, and this would be the start of the nation of Israel, the tribe set apart by God. It all started with a simple 'GO' and an obedient 'YES'. Isaac is their prize. After many years of agonising and waiting, this boy fills every void they have lived with. He is their one and only son. And then, God speaks again. He calls Abraham again, and Abraham responds this time with two Hebrew words that would change his life forever:

5 | THE YES WORD

'Hi-neni' – here I am.'[4]

God speaks again, but this time, the stakes are higher. He calls Abraham to go and take Isaac up Mt Moriah, to leave the low ground, what is familiar, and walk towards the high ground, into the uncharted and unknown. He must build an altar and then do the unthinkable: sacrifice his son, his tangible picture of the mighty nation, his promise of a future, and his symbol of blessing – his one and only son. His flesh–given as a burnt offering.

Have you ever asked yourself: *why would God do that?* I know I have.

The burnt offering was the first and most significant of all the sacrifices because it was the most costly and the most holy. God was not only asking Abraham to sacrifice his son; He was asking him to bring Him his best and give it away. It was a picture of what God would do through Jesus and what God would catalyse through the obedience of a man: a plan to rescue and redeem humanity once and for all.

The Bible can sometimes be full of gaps within the story. My vivid imagination likes to fill in the spaces with possibilities and outcomes. This story causes me to think long and hard. When I look at it from God's perspective, I partially understand what He was trying to do. However, as a parent, I have often wrestled with Abraham's response. He doesn't say a word. Not a thing is recorded. When God asks, he gets up the next morning and takes his son up a mountain journey. For days, they work together to build an altar worthy of this obedient response–something significant that could hold a growing boy. Let that sink in. I've often wondered what Abraham was thinking as he built and worked to create an altar to hold his son. Was he afraid? Or was he so sure of God's promise that he just took one step after another towards God's request? Three long days later, they are ready, and Isaac, the precious first son, asks, 'Where is the lamb, papa?' He sees everything is prepared, but there is no animal to sacrifice. When he asks his father out of a place of curiosity, Abraham confidently reminds him that God will provide what they need. The story gets more and more disturbing as he takes his son and ties him to the altar. He's about to end his child's life when an angel appears and calls his name one more time.

Abraham responds to the angel again with *'Hi-neni – Here I am'*. Here, God speaks and praises Abraham for withholding nothing from Him. For trusting Him. For being willing to give away his best. His most precious prize and possession. In what feels like a glorious turn of events, a ram suddenly appears in the thicket. A sacrifice waiting patiently to assume the role for which Isaac was intended. It is a vivid picture and prophetic declaration of how Jesus would show up for humanity.

Each time I read this story, something new enters my heart. Most recently, it was this supernatural and otherworldly idea that God always provides. He made a promise that required Isaac, but because God is faithful to Himself, He ensured He followed through on what He had promised. This story can feel far-fetched and somewhat extreme, but it is supposed to be that way. It shows us a snapshot of the extreme lengths God would go to for us. To say YES to us once more through His one and only Son. He would not stop until what He intended was finished. It would take the ultimate grand gesture and sacrifice of His own Son, Jesus, to see humanity reconciled to Himself. Again, the crux of the story is found in the humanness of the YES response. In Abraham's *'Hi-neni – Here I Am'*.

'Hi-neni' is a statement of intent.

'Tes, Tes, where are you?' 'Hineni – Here I am'. Present and ready. Available and open. Surrendered and consciously aware. 'Here I am' confirms that we are fully present in our response. Physically, mentally, emotionally, and spiritually. 'Here I am,' says I'm here, and I am willing. That was how Abraham chose to respond to God's call for him. This is how we are being asked to respond to the open doors lying before us today.

Modern-day Rabbis often unpack 'Hi-neni' as a response to the eternal question God has been asking since the very beginning.

'Where are you?' is the most challenging existential question of our day. A question that looks not for a physical location but a location of the heart. Where are you on this life's journey? Where are you going, and where do you want to end up?

It starts in the Creation Garden poem, and I believe God still asks the same question every day. He beckons us to respond to His call with a swift, present, and obedient YES, as a child responds to the call of their Father.

I once heard Abraham's 'Hi-neni' response narrated profoundly. The speaker recounted the story and passionately landed on Abraham's response with a poetic licence that gripped my heart. 'Here I am; the answer is YES before You even ask.'

When I heard those words 'YES before You even ask', I resolved within the depths of myself that I would be this woman. The girl who says YES to God before He even has to ask. The one who does unorthodox and unnatural things according to humanity and cultural norms because she knows she says YES to God, not man. The girl who chooses the road less travelled, knowing the prize is ultimately Him. The girl who lives the YES Life, an obedient life, no matter the cost.

Abraham models something beautiful. He shows us a relationship where risk and trust can co-exist. God will, indeed, ask us to do the uncomfortable. He may even call us to more than we can handle. Ultimately, however, He always makes good on what He promises. Abraham had no idea what God would ask when he responded, 'Hi-neni.'

'God is doing something magnificent in the world. When a door is opened, count the costs. Weigh up the pros and the cons. Get wise counsel. Look as far down the road as you can. But in your deepest heart, in the most secret place, have a tiny bias in the direction YES. Cultivate a willingness to charge through open doors.' – John Ortberg.[5]

I have chosen the Abraham 'Hi-neni' way. Here I am. It's YES before You even ask. It's YES without the whole picture and the entire script. It's YES without a guaranteed outcome.

Even in impossible circumstances, a YES to God is still the best YES we will ever say.

6 | When Ordinary People Say YES

Have you ever felt stirred to step up and into a moment? To say YES to something that you know needs YOU, but you don't know what to do next?

Have you ever felt prompted within a group of friends to shift the conversation, to change the narrative, to step up and into a different way? To say YES and change how those around you speak over their world, but you weren't sure your voice was enough?

Have you ever felt challenged to bring something worthwhile to your workplace at a decision-making level? Have you ever felt ready to serve your leaders with alternative strategies and ideas but couldn't find the courage to take the next step?

Have you ever felt determined to give away your best self? Have you ever contemplated giving away your talents, time, and treasure? Have you ever wanted to say YES and bring your whole self to the table? You've felt ready to step up and in, but you weren't sure you had anything of value to offer?

If you can relate, the truth is, you're one of many. Like me, who has stumbled along the road less travelled, this uncharted path may cause you to think that the great YES stories are reserved for people with that little something 'extra'. The elite or gifted types. The ones who appear to be born with supernatural skills and talents.

For many years, I believed that history-making people are unique. They must have something else going on. Perhaps they're more obedient, possibly more compliant, or maybe they have some secret power I don't have. On more than one occasion, I have excluded myself from living this audacious YES Life because I was unsure I had what it takes. I've thought that risk and bold living are 'someone else's thing' or exhilarating faith steps belong to somebody else.

I've since come to learn that the YES Life is for everyone. When I moved beyond myself and told my inner voice to quiet down, I found that the only thing getting in the way of the YES I had so long to say was **me.** In this case, I am indeed the problem.

The YES Life invites me to be a part of something significant, and at the heart of it is the realisation that it's about so much more than me. When I engage the stories within scripture or read about incredible people in history, I see a common denominator: ordinary people who just said YES.

Reading about Abraham from Paul's accounts, you will see he was not a superhuman faith carrier. He dared to believe that YES was his to say. He was dubious on many fronts, but you cannot fault his effortless ability to say YES to God. God chose Abraham. He decided to work in and through him because he said a wild and bold YES, even when it didn't make sense.

'Against all hope, Abraham in hope believed and so became the father of many nations, just as it had been said to him, "So shall your offspring be."

Without weakening in his faith, he faced the fact that his body was as good as dead – since he was about a hundred years old – and that Sarah's womb was also dead. Yet he did not waver through unbelief regarding the promise of God but was strengthened in his faith and gave glory to God, being fully persuaded that God had the power to do what he had promised.' – Romans 4: 18-21 NIV

I have an interesting make-up. I'm an A-type achiever, strategist, and all-around responsible human. I love to find solutions and fix things. Because of this, the story of Abraham lets me down. There is no step-by-step formula or strategy regarding his YES.

Abraham's wife manipulates him to bear a son through his slave. He hands Sarah over to Egyptians, pretending to be her brother. Twice. We read about his humanness. He's flawed, and he's often weak. He lacks vision and is a people pleaser. In his humanity, however, he says YES. YES to God anyway, despite himself. That's what counts more. What makes Abraham unique is that he doesn't make himself more prominent and better than he is. He makes God the hero of the story, which makes his YES significantly different.

Great YES stories have two common denominators: they contain the exceptionally 'normal' and hold a YES spirit that says, 'I am here for it.'

We hear more stories of greatness from obscure, unlikely, unqualified, broken people than from the put-together types. Brilliant things come from those who face adversity within their ordinary human stories.

The people of these ordinary stories epitomise the YES spirit. They are tenacious in their movement towards what they feel called to and believe in. They pursue YES at significant cost and risk to themselves.

History is full of stories of men and women who, from places of ordinariness, displayed a YES spirit.

Oprah Winfrey. Nelson Mandela. Queen Elizabeth I. Jim Elliot. Biddy Chambers. Jael. Deborah. Mary. David. Gideon. Joshua. Peter. Paul.

Life could have been easier. There were obstacles to overcome, pain to endure, relational discomfort, adversity, and opposition. And yet, they said YES.

These are different people with unique stories and outcomes, yet they all have humanity in common. Some were rich, and some were poor. Some were royal, and others were not. Some were black and some white. Some were male, and some were female. YES is not reserved for a specific gender, race, ethnicity, creed, or class. YES is a response every single person can bring to the table.

Oprah Winfrey was your average African-American girl. She was abused, marginalised, held back, and discriminated against. Nonetheless, she felt the pull of YES. She had a dream of being a news anchor and show host. What she dreamt of had not been done before. She said YES, again and again, even amidst significant opposition. She became the first black woman news anchor in the United States and is now one of the most prominent women in the world. The author of books, the winner of an Oscar, and the host of our generation's most famous talk show.

Nelson Mandela grew up in rural South Africa. His upbringing was difficult and unjust, with no access to running water and electricity. He had to fight to get his education. Yet, he said YES to becoming part of a great movement that fought the growing influence of Apartheid in South Africa. He knew the risks. He counted the costs. He knew the consequences, and he said YES anyway. He carried a YES spirit. His YES led to 27 years imprisonment on Robben Island. He lost precious years with his wife and didn't see his children grow up. He was forced to do mindless work, day in and day out. He said YES to sacrifice his own life and family for the sake of a belief in equality and the rights of black people. He said YES to forgiveness. When facing his oppressors, he responded with forgiveness. He will forever be remembered for choosing forgiveness over bitterness and hate. He had every reason to destroy and tear down as he rose in influence and power. Yet, throughout his leadership of South Africa, he led people towards reconciliation and peace. He led South Africa as President for five years and was one of the most influential men to walk the planet.

Queen Elizabeth I was an enigma. She used her status and position to do great things despite her gender and the pain she endured growing up. She watched her father execute her mother. She was discarded and named illegitimate. Despite her lack of authority and position, she demanded to be educated. She was known for her work ethic and sharp intellect. She said YES to leadership when men aggressively opposed women in leadership. She was not put off by the brutal threats of war and the implications of what it meant for her to reign over a patriarchal society. She said YES because she believed it was her right and calling. Her words still arrest my soul and remind me that when women say YES, profound things take place. Facing the undeniable warning that an invasion was imminent, she spoke with conviction and confidence to the people, saying: *'I may have the frail and feeble body of a woman, but I have the stomach and the heart of a King.'* [5]

Queen Elizabeth I said YES when everyone around her was saying no. She paved the way for many after her to do the same.

Jim Elliot was an ordinary young man convinced that no one should be denied the gift of the Gospel message. He said YES to going to faraway places to preach the gospel. This led him to Ecuador. He became a martyr, but his story and legacy have seen thousands of people come to know Jesus.

Gertrude Chambers was Oswald Chambers' devoted wife – also known as BD, short for Beloved Disciple. Gertrude was an ordinary girl who married an articulate, passionate preacher. She sat under his thoughts and teachings for years with just her pen and journal. After his death, she was disturbed by the reality that his messages would die with him. She said YES to remain anonymous and ensure the legacy of her husband's work was presented to the world. BD wrote every book that we read today, which was recorded to have been written by Oswald Chambers. Her YES is the gold in 'My Utmost for His Highest.' I often look at this profound story and wonder what would have happened if she had wanted the recognition and fame for herself. What would have happened if she hadn't faithfully shown up and taken notes sermon after sermon? Would Oswald Chambers even exist in our minds if his wife hadn't so wholeheartedly believed in him? It's amazing what happens when we don't care about who gets the credit.

Everywhere you look, ordinary people have said YES to something great. Their YES has paved the way for something magical to happen around them.

When ordinary people say YES, miracles happen.
When ordinary people say YES, others are set free.
When ordinary people say YES, governments change.
When ordinary people say YES, social injustice is overcome.
When ordinary people say YES, cycles of abuse are disrupted.
When ordinary people say YES, they are called to walk into their destiny and purpose.
When ordinary people say YES, people are ushered into better days than they ever dreamed.
When ordinary people say YES, the impossible becomes possible.
When ordinary people say YES, it inspires others to say YES, too.
When ordinary people say YES, it opens doors for others to find their way home.

When we stand up and respond with 'YES, no matter what, God, the answer is YES, before You even ask.' The atmosphere changes, and miracles happen. A big YES to God will always usher in the supernatural and miraculous. God is in the mighty business of taking our human YES and transferring His power into responses that partner with Him.

I believe that I am that ordinary girl. Some may look at my accomplishments and the highlight reel of my life and think that there is something special, and perhaps there is. It's just not what you think. I am not a genius and don't have an abnormally high IQ. I don't hold some rare or unique talent. I am not from a bloodline of royalty, nor do

I hold anything that elevates me within the influential parts of society. The extraordinary secret power you think I may have is also available for you. It's one small word. The readiness to respond to God's ask with a 'YES, before I know what the outcome will be.'

I have resolved within the depths of my heart and soul to err on the side of YES when it comes to the prompts and lead of the Holy Spirit.

As I take stock of my short life, I can confidently say that my YES to God has taken me to places I never dreamt I could go and continues to surprise me even today.

A Note

Hi.

I hope you're making sense of The YES Life so far.

Throughout the following chapters, I want to help you see how saying YES to God enabled me to say YES more than I ever knew I needed.

My YES to Him unlocked a YES to marriage, children, women, pain, Church, leadership, and more.

I pray that a word or a phrase will meet you on your journey and in your season.

I hope that YES will become your story, too.

That every no will be turned around.
That every wall would be torn down.
That every lie would be uncovered.
That every obstacle be cast into the depths of the sea.

Would you begin to see and hear what YES you need to say and what doors you need to walk through boldly?

I believe in you.

A Prayer for the YES Waiting before You

God,

As we read and engage these words, would You reveal, heal and clearly show each of us the way through.

Give us courage and lead us on this road less travelled. Grant us the boldness to move bravely forward. Guide our YES as you guide us home.

Amen.

7 | YES to God

I wasn't the one to say YES first. You get that now, right? God always makes the first move. He made a grand gesture towards me. He stretched out His gracious hand. He reached out. He held nothing back, so I could say a resounding YES to Him in return.

I think it's essential to distinguish between saying YES to God and YES to what He wants us to do. I've repeatedly said YES to what He wants me to do, but there has only been one distinct moment where I said YES to Him and Him alone.

As a young girl, I spent a year in the United Kingdom after school, travelling and exploring. That year embedded within me great confidence and independence. It also saw me letting my hair down in ways a young 18-year-old can do. This was my self-proclaimed rite of passage into adulthood. I left my mark in Europe in a few questionable ways, and to this day, I am grateful that, at this point, social media did not exist. I came home, thankfully, after 11 months and followed my boyfriend, now husband, to Stellenbosch University. There, I continued to find myself in unhelpful situations at significant cost to myself and those I loved. I had an unhealthy relationship with my body, and alcohol gave me the false courage I needed to feel worthy of people's attention. I was insecure and looked for attention in all the wrong places.

Later that year, the same boyfriend gave his heart and life to Jesus. He said YES to God. I will forever be grateful that I got to witness the miracle of his life transformation. Looking back, it was almost as if his life changed overnight. Gone were the parties. Gone were the crazy habits and reckless days. In their place were long days beside a river on his own with his Bible and Hillsong United worship songs. He had found a new friend. He was excited and alive. I, however, was confused and felt left out. When a travelling preacher came to Dylan's church, I followed along to see what this newfound relationship with God was all about. The man preaching was enormous. Enigmatic. I was intrigued. I'll never forget how I fought the instinct to run. He walked up to me after the message, looked me in the eyes and said: '*Young woman, God has given you a blank page. Will you say YES to Him?*'

I was so overwhelmed by this point I nodded and prayed a prayer that someone prompted me to pray. It was the beginning of my salvation story, but I felt a nagging pressure to do what my boyfriend did, hoping to salvage what was left of our relationship. I responded to what I thought would fix us instead of saying YES because He was calling me. I realised the fear of letting go of my relationship prompted my response that night. I didn't know what and to whom I was saying YES. As it happened, I compromised this YES and lost the relationship with him anyway.

In hindsight, I will forever be grateful for this moment of real heartbreak.

I had lost everything I thought I couldn't live without. Dylan was my past, present, and future in that season of my life. I could not

7 | YES TO GOD

fathom life without him, and now, here I was, because of my failure and decisions, forced to consider a life that looked different from the one I had imagined. One afternoon, I was sitting with a friend going on and on about my broken heart when she promptly looked at me and said:

'Tes, do you want me to tell you the truth? You don't need Dylan to have a beautiful and brave life. He will never fully satisfy you. He can not. You must build a life that is true to yourself and what God is calling you to. If Dylan is part of that plan, it will happen. Move on. Live your life.'

As I grappled with my loss, I took her words to heart and did the only thing I could think: I ran towards the One who had offered me a blank page, a new story, and a life full of Him.

I remember kneeling in my room one desperate night because the physical pain of the loss was taking my breath away. My life was a mess. I was sick. I was alone. I was addicted to ways of coping that were destroying my soul. As I cried out to Him to rescue what was left of me, I clung to this otherworldly trust that He would turn my life around and heal my heart from the inside out.

I ran towards God's presence and said YES to Him. I wasn't saying YES to God so He'd give me my boyfriend back. I was saying YES to God because this gaping hole in my heart felt impossibly large, and something inside told me it was a void that only God would fill.

I woke up the following day with what can only be described as fresh breath in my lungs. My eyes felt bright, and my heart was full of peace.

'Weeping comes in the night, but joy will come in the morning.' ⁷

He did it like only He can.
He'd healed so much of my physical pain and harmful behaviour as I slept overnight.
He met me in my deep ache.
He bridged the gap my lifestyle and decisions had put between myself and my God.
He soothed my raw parts that were desperate to be seen and known.
He ushered in kindness and peace to the depths of my anxious heart.
He restored order and removed all the destructive habits and behaviour I had been conditioned to.
He gave me new energy and a fresh perspective.
Everything suddenly felt vibrant and alive.
Life felt possible again.

My past wasn't overwhelming, and the prospect of saying goodbye to the only man I truly loved no longer made me anxious.
I felt life beating through my veins.
I saw my smile return.
I saw my true self for the first time in years.
I was happy. I had joy.

'Once, I was dead, but now I am alive.'[8]

I dived head-first into a relationship with God and His word. I was fascinated by His heart and wanted to understand His ways. I wanted to know more. In my exploration, I encountered this uncomfortable idea that saying YES to God meant saying YES to obedience.

7 | YES TO GOD

And I started to wonder. What if YES and obedience meant life in abundance?

What if YES to God was a matter of perspective and vision rather than a life of restriction?

8 | YES to Marriage

I was about to turn 22. My life was at a significant crossroads. Instinctively, I knew everything that followed in the next few years would mark me in ways I couldn't begin to understand. I felt like I was waiting for this epic race in the starting blocks, but nobody was shooting the start gun.

Dylan and I seemed yet again to be at a defining point in our relationship. Dating was hard. We could not draw the physical boundary lines. Going after purity meant more time apart, which presented other challenges. We were playing this tap dancing game around the reality of our present and the uncertainty of our future. It was an odd time. I wanted to start a forever story, but I still longed for many things that I didn't think fit within marriage and being a wife. I had dreams of stages and performing. My studies were ending, and I longed to pursue the arts and music. I began to seek opportunities overseas, but I knew if he asked me to marry him, I wouldn't be able to turn that down. I would say YES, even if it meant giving up on some of my dreams. I knew a YES to marriage was what I wanted, but I didn't entirely understand what this YES truly meant, and I was about to be taught about the art of surrender.

Dylan had asked to picnic on our farm in a remote, idyllic space where a natural rock form became a waterfall. It is still, to this day, one of the most beautiful places in the world. I didn't fully understand his want to be alone. *Were we not trying to avoid being alone at all costs?* We didn't ordinarily hang out together like this, so my heart fluttered with anticipation; my expectations of a proposal were low, especially as he had articulated he wasn't ready for marriage and believed I wasn't either.

My nerves eased as I stepped into my safe place in the heart of the Glendale Valley. There was just something about the sound of running water mixed with the cry of a Crowned Eagle flying above us. I was at home there. I was at peace there. This was where I'd kissed him as a 15-year-old, still trying to understand why this one boy had such an effect on me, and six years later, the memory of us as kids still made me smile. Our relationship was mysterious and baffling, yet being with him in that place felt right. It felt good.

Dylan has always been one for words. He caught my attention as he started to tell me the things he loved about us specifically. The way I made him feel and the future he saw. Within a few moments, the dream he shared with me made my heart come alive. 'Can you imagine it?' he asked, and before I could respond, he held a ring, saying, 'I think we are forever. I just need your YES.'

Fast-forward five months to a crisp autumn day on the North Coast of KZN. I was dressed in white with my dream-long veil, surrounded by friends and family. I was about to step into a quaint Anglican chapel where we currently attended church, and my parents had married 22 years earlier. That day, I wasn't nervous anymore. I was sure. I wanted to say YES, to confidently choose this forever and move onwards and upwards into our adventure together.

We were still kids as we looked into each other's eyes and promised big, audacious things. To cherish. To hold. To love. To honour and respect. To fight for each other and journey alongside one another. In the good times and healthy times. In the hard times and sick times. Whether we had money or not. Whether we felt like it or not. We said YES, but, quite frankly, at the tender age of 22 and 24, we had no idea what saying YES to marriage would ultimately mean and how much this YES would demand from us.

Saying YES does not mean the road will be without hurdles and bumps. I tell my children more often than they want to hear that nothing worthwhile comes easily. Just because we chose marriage did not mean there would be no challenges or heartache.

Saying YES to marriage has been the best yet most challenging YES I have ever said.

Our marriage has been a beautiful and messy journey of facing ourselves and one another. Year after year after year. We were young and in love. We had no idea what it meant to lay down our lives for each other. We were idealistic, and our expectations were worlds apart. What does that look like over time? We are consistently bridging the gap between our expectations and reality. We have had to figure out what it means to love when we don't feel like it. To offer our bodies when we would rather roll over onto the other side of the bed. To bring all of ourselves to the table – even the ugliest unspoken parts – so that love would cover it all.

I thought saying YES once on a bright August day would be enough. However, being married, I realised I had to choose to say YES again every day.

YES, I choose you.

YES, I love you.

YES, I respect you.

YES, I honour you.

YES, I put you before myself.

YES, I forgive you.

YES, I will share it with you.

YES, to friendship.

YES, to sacrifice.

YES, to someone else's preference.

YES, to listening.

YES, to build someone else's vision and dream.

YES, to a partnership.

YES, I see you.

YES, I need you.

YES, it is you and only you.

In today's post-modern, comfort-driven culture, we often blur the lines when we say YES to meet our personal preferences. Saying YES to marriage is much more than saying YES to a life partner. Of course, it is a big part of it, and it matters that we come alongside another person wholeheartedly. We also, however, say YES to championing their hearts and blowing wind into their sails. We choose to cheer them on to become the best version of themselves. We say YES to who they are, even when we don't agree on everything. We say YES to the many chapters of life they will go through as individuals. We say YES to witnessing every change and shift within them. Marriage is one thing when you're tangled in each other's arms, whispering declarations of love and adoration. It's sweet when you're on the mountaintop of togetherness. But what happens when you are disappointed by your spouse or when they hurt you deeply? What happens when they fail to show up and tread upon your heart? What happens when they betray your trust and choose themselves over your well-being? Do we say YES, even then?

Saying YES to marriage goes beyond another person. Saying YES to marriage moves beyond the tangible nature of humanness and takes us into supernatural and spiritual places. This is the place where faith is accessed, and trust is everything. Where we decide YES before the hard times come. When the storms rage, and we have exhausted every option and avenue of healing, we lean into the faith we need to keep moving on through.

Side note: If you're reading this and your marriage ended because the reality of your togetherness with another person was beyond repair and utterly damaging to your health and wholeness, please be free. Don't hear what I am not saying. Remove the shame off of yourself. Marriages do end, sometimes necessarily. Even in that ending, there is grace upon grace for YOU. There is hope for your healing and a new day for your life.

Saying YES to marriage means living *naked and unashamed* before another human. It's a YES to bear your soul and trust that you will be loved, even if you are broken and unlovely in seasons.

Saying YES to marriage looks like uncovering shame around intimacy and learning about someone else's body and mind.

Saying YES to marriage includes the willingness to communicate our wants and needs.

Saying YES to marriage includes trusting that our spouse will nurture what has been entrusted to them over time.

Saying YES to marriage includes the willingness to give away our best for someone else to thrive.

Saying YES to marriage looks like saying sorry when you're wrong and also when you're right.

Saying YES to marriage looks like leveraging everything to see someone else's heart set on fire.

Saying YES to marriage means going on a journey of becoming your best self.

The Bible calls marriage a mystery, and this is why most people fail to sum it up in all its parts. It's the most breathtakingly sacrificial YES we will say every day, and yet, it is also the sweetest.

I don't know how it's happened, but over time, we've stumbled upon who we are together in our human attempt to be married. It's better. Dylan and I are dynamic alone. Both of us are called and capable. We have vision. Alone and apart, we can live with unrivalled passion. We know how to get on with it and make our way. However, in our togetherness, we seem to excel even more. We fight against our independence because it's when we're interdependent that there is momentum, ease, and flow.

When I said YES to marriage, I had no idea I was saying YES to living in the mystery of unity and partnership. A living, breathing picture of God.

'If you've gotten anything at all out of following Christ, if his love has made any difference in your life, if being in a community of the Spirit means anything to you, if you have a heart if you care – then do me a favour: Agree with each other, love each other, be deep-spirited friends. Don't push your way to the front; don't sweet-talk your way to the top. Put yourself aside and help others get ahead. Don't be obsessed with getting your own advantage. Forget yourselves long enough to lend a helping hand.' – Philippians 2:1-8 MSG

In a nutshell, say YES to each other. Choose and prefer each other day by day by day.

We choose each other over ourselves.
We choose intimacy over isolation.
We choose friendship over function.

Years back, we started using a phrase we coined from Hillsong Church, 'Better together.' It sounded good, and it had an inviting ring to it. We positioned it in the middle of everything we did across our organisation. What it built was this dynamic belief system and culture that communicated how we can go fast alone, but together, we can go far.

'Better together' looks like finishing the race with a friend. We've made it a value in our home that reminds our kids that we may be good alone, but together, we could possibly be great. Dylan and I have unique gifting, roles, and expectations. We are exquisitely different. But, when we size up our differences and harness our strengths together, you will find a formidable team.

Mother Theresa says, *'I can do things you cannot do, you can do things I cannot do, and together we can do great things.'*

9 | YES to Children

I was sitting with a new gynaecologist, and I didn't like this conversation. I didn't like her.

'*I need to prepare you for the worst,*' she said.

This doctor was not holding anything back, and her bedside manner left much to be desired. She wasn't the first. This was the third doctor I had seen in a year, and they had all painted a pretty grim picture of my childbearing future. I was scared and angry. *At 22 years old, how was this conversation even happening?* She gave me two choices. I could start trying for a baby early on in our marriage, and if it took years, we'd be young enough to cope with the wait. Or, we could wait until it was convenient to start 'trying' and then be in for a possible infertility journey that I didn't want to face.

I felt like I was stuck between a rock and a hard place. My five-year plan seemed solid: finish my degree, get a great job, travel, and be married. It certainly did not include a baby yet. Of course, I loved the idea of children – two children with a dog and a white fence, to be exact. What if I let nature take its course and immediately became pregnant? And if not, did I have the patience and stamina to face infertility?

I didn't know what I wanted. I loved my five-year plan. It felt dependable and stable. It looked great on paper; everyone else did it that way. The problem was it just didn't feel right. It seemed like God Himself was whispering into the deep recesses of my heart. 'Will you trust me?'

I told some friends, and their response was, 'You're crazy! You're 22! There is no rush!' The human voices around us weren't wrong; they were calculated and cautious. Still, this gentle, provoking invitation was within me to say YES. To trust God with my life, all of it. To surrender even my five-year plan. To believe that His future for me was good, pleasing and perfect even when it looked so different from my plans. To lean further into this bizarre yet fundamental belief that God's ways are higher than mine and often don't make sense.

One night, as I crept into the perfect space between Dylan's chin and shoulder, I shared what was within me. I shared with him that waiting seemed scarier than a baby outside of my plan and that I wanted to be open to whatever God had for us, whether it be one month, eight months, two years, or ten years. I wanted the freedom to respond with a YES and see what happens.

My YES to God and His call to family became a beautiful blurry mess of three baby girls, one exuberant son, a full heart, and an even fuller home. I do, still to this day, have issues that could have hindered my ability to fall pregnant, but for some reason, my body defied science. It seemed as though Dylan and I could look at each other, and children kept creeping into our lives and hearts. But there is more to this story.

Some years later, as I juggled carpool, nappies, homework, and the relentless nature of small children, the miracle of children became familiar. It's amazing how time can dull the brilliance of a miracle story. The value of family is hard work when placed at the pinnacle of priority. Even if it is indeed a miracle, it can be challenging. Let that sink in. Even miracles can call for everything from within us. It takes a lot to keep living with the conviction that I can love and lead my family, nurture my children, and, at the same time, build and lead within the local church. The belief that we should take our kids on this journey of life and ministry with us is one of the best YESES I have ever said. And it all started when I moved beyond my five-year plan, two children, a dog and a white picket fence.

In 2016, in an overwhelmed state, I landed in the USA, excited for the opportunity to travel. Leaving the children behind always came with a lot of sacrifice and organisation. I arrived in America unsure about what I was doing and where I was going. This trip seemed strangely significant, yet the fatigue and the stretch of travel were evident as my body demanded I go slower and steadier. In high-placed seats, I sat in a room of thousands of people at the Hillsong Conference and sank into the moment's mindblowing creativity. The imagery showcased what happens when we live our lives hurried and oblivious. It highlighted to me that if we are not careful, we can land in the land of forgetfulness. Living lives devoid of vision, hope, clarity, and purpose. I certainly did not want this life. I craved the God-breathed life I knew was mine to have in Jesus. Somehow, though, here I was, having lost my memory, and I had to travel to New York City to remember again.

As the music faded, we sat in glorified silence. I began to journal my thoughts to be ever-present and committed to this moment.

I wrote: *'In the future, God, I see myself holding a baby.'*

Wait. What?

'God, I think you're asking me to have another child. I believe there is more.'
More from my body. More from my marriage. More from my YES?
Another child? I have three **ALREADY**.
Is this You, God?
Have you not seen how I am dropping all the balls in my life?
Have you noticed the fatigue?
What about our marriage? We don't have any time for each other. What would another child bring?
Is this you, God? Or am I losing my mind?

I was fighting what I was sensing, but looking back, I knew this was God. I just knew.

As the days went by, the gentle whisper kept pulling at my heart, asking me to respond once more to what seemed humanly impossible of my capacity.

I have realised that sometimes our YES leads us to places we need to go, but it doesn't often look like we expected. We did fall pregnant.

We were excited. Expectant.

But it didn't turn out the way you may think. I lost the sweet baby I'd imagined in New York after just 15 weeks.

9 | YES TO CHILDREN

To begin to articulate the pain of a miscarriage is a story in itself.

I was devastated. Did I not hear God? Was I wrong? Getting out of bed in the morning was hard. I would hide away in the early hours most days to weep secretly on the bathroom floor. I didn't feel this pain could be entrusted to the people around me, so I shared it with the only One I knew who could hold it.

I felt so disillusioned. I had willed myself to YES, believing in the invitation to have more children. Why did this happen? And where was God now?

This YES hurt. I just could not understand it. Had I not heard God? Again, I reconciled that living a safe, more calculated life was better. The life where YES was orchestrated and only said when I could control and manipulate the outcome. I didn't know how to walk through this moment well. I hid so much of the pain, choosing to ignore it, but God's grace and kindness allowed me to unravel, little by little, and through this, I would find greater healing on the other side.

He allowed me the privilege of that pain so that I would uncover more of His Heart. He would set me up for strength and resilience as I walked through one of the most severe seasons of my life. It was rough and lonely, but He came with me. He stood close. He held my heart. He would generously and swiftly take me on an adventure to where Jesus Himself walked and show me more and more of His grace.

A year later, I was overseas again. The Holy Land, Israel. I was excited to be there, but I was somewhat numb. My miscarriage had caused me to become strangely anxious. Leaving my children was not only complicated, but it pulled the rug of my self-made security from under me. The media had painted a hostile picture of this contested biblical land, and I was nervous about the constant threat of war.

As the plane circled this small God-ordained land, I saw the ground below me, and my heart began to beat faster as I felt it crack open and shift. I had no idea what God would do, but I anticipated I would never be the same again.

This trip to Israel epitomised magnificence. God's extravagance met my heart on every street corner, reminding me that the land of forgetfulness was not the existence He had planned for me. He had brought me to Israel to remember.

Pomegranates, the fruit representing vitality and fertility, dripped from bushes on the side of the road. I had received so many pictures and words of encouragement from people in the past about this fruit and what it represents in my life. Seeing it fall at my feet reminded me that the Father sees all. He loved my heart in personal ways that I will never forget. This trip was the one where I began to trust purposefully again. Hope slowly grew with each new day.

We found ourselves at the healing Baths of Bethesda just a few days before leaving. The Baths overlook where the lame man sat below the 'Gate Beautiful'. To be fair, I was in myself lame at the Gate Beautiful. Standing before all the possibilities to come, but disillusioned with my 'YES'. I felt just like that lame man lying at the pool. I hoped angels

9 | YES TO CHILDREN

would swirl the waters that could heal and one of my travel mates would be kind enough to throw me inside. As the story goes with Peter, John, and the lame man, our tour leader found me lying on my mat staring at the water. He pulled me aside and gave me not what I thought I needed but rather what Jesus held.

His words of truth and compassion over the baby I had lost two months earlier allowed the hardy exterior I'd created around my heart to shatter. As he repurposed my pain and engaged in the reality of my brokenness, the tears began to flow. The kind of tears that heal. The ones that God Himself bottles up and stores for Himself. In this holy, unscripted moment, he asked me to look over the healing baths towards the homes on the other side. There, across the way, was the home of Horation Spafford.

Horatio sent his wife and four daughters on a voyage across the Atlantic in search of a better quality of life for his family in the 1800s. Tragically, the ship didn't make the journey and was hit by a Scottish vessel. Every single one of his children died, and only his wife survived. In an attempt to rebuild his life, he moved with his wife a few years later to Jerusalem to serve the Jewish people. There, overlooking the healing Baths of Bethesda, people believe he wrote *'It Is Well With My Soul.'*

'When peace like a river, attendeth my way
When sorrows like sea billows roll
Whatever my lot, thou hast taught me to say
It is well, it is well, with my soul
It is well

With my soul
It is well, it is well with my soul

Though Satan should buffet, though trials should come
Let this blest assurance control
That Christ has regarded my helpless estate
And hath shed His blood for my soul

It is well (it is well)
With my soul (with my soul)
It is well, it is well with my soul

My sin, oh, the bliss of this glorious thought!
My sin, not in part but the whole
Is nailed to the cross, and I bear it no more
Praise the Lord, praise the Lord, o my soul!

It is well (it is well)
With my soul (with my soul)
It is well, it is well with my soul
It is well (it is well)
With my soul (with my soul)
It is well, it is well with my soul.[9]

This profound placement of a house, a song and a story written overlooking the healing Baths was not lost on me. We walked into an ancient church with the best natural acoustics in the Northern Hemisphere. I felt the atmosphere shift in my heart because I knew I was here, not by chance, but because God would not leave me confused by

9 | YES TO CHILDREN

my YES. Our tour leader asked if anyone could sing. I shrunk low into my seat at the possibility of singing for my tour group.

'Tes sings!' I heard someone say at the back.

He looked at me with kind eyes and said: *'I think you should sing 'It is well with my soul.'*

It's difficult for me to explain what happened in that chapel on the other side of the world on a blistering hot day in Jerusalem. It's impossible to recreate that moment for you as I write. I so desperately want to because I feel like it was a moment I want everyone to experience. It was a moment where my loss was seen and validated.

I had arrived lame, lying at the gate like the man who called out to Peter and John. Like him, I had been asking people for something they could not give me. But God knew what I needed. I needed to acknowledge the loss. I needed to make peace with this notion that sometimes our *'YES'* can be painful and costly. But it's still worthwhile and vital to be said. I could let my sorrow go as I sang the words of someone who knew greater depths of loss and agony, allowing his words to encourage my soul again. At that moment, I promised God I would not close my heart to more babies, to that little fourth being that I had imagined in New York years before. I'd keep saying YES and vulnerably trust Him with that YES once more.

A year later, I failed to update my ovulation tracking app. I soon realised that my inability to stay awake past 7 pm, my sudden aversion to coffee and my craving for cake and mussel chowder was the beautiful beginning of Joel. The child Dylan prayed for at Shiloh on the same trip to Israel. Unbeknownst to me, my husband knew my heart was closed to another child. He asked God to give him a miracle: a wife with a healed heart and a son.

God worked out my YES and Dylan's desires without any work or effort on our behalf. That's how good He is. That is the power of YES.

10 | YES to Church

My biggest concerns about the church were based on the 'warnings' I received from people in existing church work positions.

'Pastor's kids don't tend to turn out so well.'
'Church tends to damage children.'
'Ministry and marriage is a difficult path.'
and *'Pastor's kids become rebellious.'*

These were repetitive statements that well-meaning pastors and friends had given me as a new mother in ministry. Whenever I heard something negative about my soon-to-be-growing family, I became agitated and stressed. I just could not partner with this narrative. I struggled to speak up and lacked the confidence, security, and trust to know that God loves them more than I do. His plans and purposes for my children far exceed what I could ever give them or even dream of for them. He is a good Father, more than I could imagine. I needed to reach a place where I could take hold of His promises for my family and truly know that we are in His good hands.

I have an affinity for my lounge carpet. It's soft and wide. It calls for kneeling, praying, and getting low in response to God 'just because' of who He is. It asks me to worship. My carpet often ushers me to sit with the only One who knows what is going on in my heart, who can lead me closer to Him all the way home.

In the early years of ministry, on a quiet, warm Durban winter's afternoon, I was wrestling with my YES to fully commit to partnering with Dylan in building the church together. In hindsight, I see how people's thoughts and words had created a story I was telling myself. I said to myself that church work was too great a risk because I felt like perhaps my children were at stake. I believed that this would come at a great cost to them, and I didn't know if this was a price I was willing to pay. A good friend once encouraged us to count the cost and acknowledge what would be necessary to build the tower. This tower could be a business, a vocation, growing a family, or building a house. He encouraged us to ask if we had what it took to build and finish the tower. As I contemplated the tower, the church I was being asked to build, I knelt before God in worship while songs of hope and courage filled the room. Oceans, by Hillsong, began to play.

'You call me out upon the waters
The great unknown where feet may fail
And there I find You in the mystery

In oceans deep my faith will stand
And I will call upon Your Name
And keep my eyes above the waves

When oceans rise
My soul will rest in Your embrace

For I am Yours and You are mine

Your grace abounds in deepest waters
Your sovereign hand will be my guide
Where feet may fail and fear surrounds me
You've never failed and You won't start now

So I will call upon Your Name
And keep my eyes above the waves

When oceans rise
My soul will rest in Your embrace
For I am Yours and You are mine, oh
And You are mine, oh

Spirit lead me where my trust is without borders
Let me walk upon the waters
Wherever You would call me
Take me deeper than my feet could ever wander
And my faith will be made stronger
In the presence of my Saviour[10]

On my lounge carpet that day, it felt like all of Heaven was beckoning me to step out. To step up and step into my YES once more.

It was not a message in the clouds. It was a gentle whisper of the Spirit moving through my heart, a tug towards YES. And I felt it. I sensed my Father's words drowning out the words previously spoken.

'Build my church, Tes.'
'Give yourself away. Every day. Give your best self to build her, and I promise I will build your house. If you take responsibility for my house, I'll build yours. If you care for my family, I will care for yours.'

Had I heard this before? Had I read it or seen it? Was it my imagination, or was this Scripture and the Spirit Himself? Was this Heaven giving me a life-giving word to hold onto? I could handle whatever came my way if I had His Word. His Word trumps every human spoken word. His promises began to leap from the pages in 2 Samuel:
'Establish a home for God Himself to dwell in, and the Earthly positions and kingdoms will reign forever.' [11]

I felt what can only be described as perfect peace that day. I knew God would not leave me. He is faithful to Himself and true to His word. We can expect Him to follow through. He is faithful, even when we are not. He cannot deny Himself. This is the confidence I needed to embark on a new journey of leading in the church, leading like we had not seen it done before. Man and woman together.

On that rug, I said YES.

'I'll build your house, Lord. I'm holding You to Your faithfulness, that as I build Yours, You will build mine. Not just the physical house and the shelter I need for each season but the legacy, lineage, influence and prosperity that I know is layered within the truth of these words. A promise of Your faithfulness towards my family for generations to come.'

In 2014, with three little girls in our home and a new church building on the brink of opening, I became a full-time pastor and leader. It was a new day, a new dawn, with fresh grace that came with it. I was expectant and excited about all God would do through a man, a woman, and a house.

11 | YES to Leadership

I had big dreams as a little girl. The world seemed to be my oyster at the tender age of nine years old. I used to watch this programme as a young girl called 'Touched by an Angel.' I dreamt that my life would hold a miraculous story. One episode enlightened my naive South African heart to the reality of the slaves in Sudan. I knew very little of slavery or slaves, but through this TV show, I became aware of slavery in North Africa. I was horrified. As you may have guessed, I was furious at the injustice, and I began to dream of rescuing slaves. I lived on a farm in a privileged reality in the proverbial middle of nowhere. What did I think I was going to do? In Grade five, we were asked to write a page about our job one day and what we wanted to be when we grew up. Saving slaves seemed like a good thing to say.

When asked, 'What do you want to be when you grow up?' I never answered with 'the Pastor's wife'. Even as a young girl, I wanted my own identity and life story. I craved significance and boldly believed my life could leave a legacy. Being labelled 'someone's wife' didn't fit my dream's picture.

Yet, here I was. 23. Married. Pregnant and labelled. A Pastor's wife. I am somewhat embarrassed to admit that I lived permanently offended at this point. Whenever someone used the title 'Pastor's wife' to introduce me, I was visibly insulted. It got underneath my skin and gnawed at my mind and heart. How and what had led me here? I never agreed to this. This title. I felt this worldly identity confined me to a space and reality that was stifling and unrealistic. I never asked for it. I had not appointed myself as 'Pastor's wife', so why was I here? And how could I possibly escape?

It's funny looking back at how indignant I was. I do apologise if you ever encountered 20-something Tes. I wish I could have had the maturity and wisdom to lighten up and let go of the titles that had held me hostage back then. If I were secure, this wouldn't have been an issue. I could have, confidently and with kindness, helped people shift from the traditions of old that have kept so many women paralysed and silent. Sadly, I wasn't any of the above, so my anger and disdain for the label and all it placed upon me drove my behaviour and responses. This had a significant effect on my marriage, my family, and the church.

After our sabbatical in 2011, I saw how I had allowed my insecurities to harm my relationship with the church and my calling. I'd purposefully run from the passion I knew I held to see people restored and healed. I'd run from the little girl within me who wanted to see slaves set free. I'd silenced and closed myself off to the vehicle, the church.

I'd run because I allowed my offence towards a title to get in the way of the actual assignment God had given me. Leadership within the church.

In all of this wrestling around my involvement and role within the church, we felt we had to go and see all the phenomenon that was Hillsong Australia. We had been following the global worship

11 | YES TO LEADERSHIP

movement for years and were excited to experience the church behind the music we loved. We saw God in it and wanted to associate ourselves with something full of audacious faith and big life.

We had said YES to marriage, YES to family and YES to taking our kids on the journey. We had said YES to church together. And so, as you do, we took every bit of savings, maxed out our credit card, sold everything we didn't need, and boarded a plane to Sydney, Australia. Four weeks. Two families. Six adults. Four kids, one nine-month-old baby, and one baby not yet born. Ten suitcases. Three prams. Five car chairs and a whole lot of blind faith.

We visited six Hillsong Churches in one month. We attended a week-long conference. We travelled for hours on planes, cars, trains, and buses. We stayed in every kind of accommodation you can imagine. We ate out. We ate in. We drank great coffee. We bathed our kids in hotel basins. We napped in parks. We dealt with a horrendous stomach bug. We threw soiled clothes in the bin and bought more on the fly. We lost a child at the conference, only to find her sleeping under a bench. We had pep talks with our team about finishing strong and digging deep. We fought with our spouses. We secretly yelled at our kids. We cried. We laughed. We celebrated and strategised. It was the wildest, most challenging and beautiful moment of my life.

In this place, God began to speak, and once more, the whisper of Heaven invited me to do something I had avoided for a season: to lead as Tes. To lay my life down and lead people within the church, the thing Jesus loves most. I put aside my preferences and aligned myself with my husband's vision to pioneer the church in a new way, where men and women lead together.

Somewhere along the way, I had allowed people's jaded opinions around church to colour the way I looked at it myself. The world and other people's preferences relating to church had blurred what seemed so simple to me. My ongoing frustration at what man called me had potentially derailed my conviction that I was born to build the church. Jesus' bride. I had allowed things to become complex in my mind, and my role had become something I was fighting so hard for rather than stepping boldly towards.

Being at the Hillsong Conference affirmed that I am called to lead. It confirmed that I could lead in the church as a woman, wife, and mother. It wasn't only an option; it was vital. When I saw a new way at Hillsong Australia, I realised my hesitation was not the answer. My authentic self could shift how people engaged with the church and related to its leaders, particularly women.

I know I don't fit the mould of your traditional 'Pastor's wife' or Pastor. If you've met me, I know you've thought it.

I'm gentle yet also opinionated. I am fierce about something I believe in, like the family unit, children and women's value in society. I may be on the smaller side and feminine, but I am often big and loud in my approach to life, particularly when getting things done. I believe that God has called me to be a minister to men and women; it's what He has anointed me for. I am honest, often to a fault, especially when I see what I think are obvious solutions to problems. I fight for a better way, which is sometimes tiring for people. I often tire myself out.

11 | YES TO LEADERSHIP

In Australia, I saw that women were both strong in leadership and utterly secure in their womanhood. Their roles of leadership flowed supernaturally within marriage and motherhood. I wanted what I saw. They could hold in both hands the realities of life that I was trying so desperately to keep separate and ordered. They called each other, men and women Pastors, and they carried a spirit of humility and openness that I knew was the answer to all the brokenness I saw in women within the South African church. I saw men championing women as they led, preached, prayed, and prophesied, and then I saw women do the same in return. I saw this church playing the best gift for each circumstance. They were not concerned about gender when fulfilling what needed to be done. This trip unlocked a new way of thinking. At that moment, God asked me, with a clarion call, to build a church and lead as a woman.

The desire to see slaves set free was not a far-fetched childish dream. God planted a seed in my heart at the tender age of nine. He would use my tenacity, fierceness, femininity, and strength to help many people find freedom in Him. I could say YES to move past my resentment toward a title and fight for a new kind of narrative for women in the church. I could pioneer a new way of leadership in the church in my generation.

The invitation was one to rise and lead. I was being asked to pick up the mantle lying on the floor before me and step into the fullness of God's calling. There was a supernatural transfer happening. I needed to take hold of it and move bravely forward again, letting go of what was and stepping into the new.

12 | YES to Women

'If you want to lift up humanity, empower women. It is the most comprehensive, pervasive, high-leverage investment you can make in human beings.' – Melinda Gates.[12]

Do you believe in divine appointments? Encounters that you know will radically affect your life? You know they're special because you had nothing to do with making them happen. They seem coincidental, but when you look back, there was nothing random about them.

I've had many such encounters. One such moment was at the Colour Conference in 2014. I'd met Lucinda Dooley a few weeks prior. In her genuinely generous and inclusive way, she urged me to come to Colour and bring three friends. We would be hosted and taken care of, and, for the first time, I would have the privilege of being in a room full of women led by Bobbie Houston. I was excited and honoured to be invited but nervous about what this moment meant for my future.

The conference was spectacular. It was unique in its creativity. Bold, yet sensitive to the whispers of the Holy Spirit. We were in a room of 4,000 women, but I felt like I was sitting in the home of some girls who loved Jesus and His Church and wanted to tell others all about it. I was awakened to this powerful and otherworldly thing that happens when women gather. I sat captivated, watching woman after woman lead and minister–calmly, confidently, and passionately. I did not know women like this, and I had never seen men rally around the feminine heart with such enthusiasm and ease. It was unfamiliar to me and I wanted it. This moment stirred something within me. I could feel the beginning of God calling my heart towards leading a movement of women in my world.

I wasn't particularly excited about the idea of women's ministry. Flowers, sentimentalities, formalities. I had tried to create gatherings and even named them Flourish, Nourish, Lavish, Cherish. There were creative moments, talks about value and position, fashion demonstrations, and dream boards. I'd attempted everything I thought women would subscribe to at Linc church, but I always felt like something was lacking. They weren't wrong. I just longed for more.

I knew God wanted more for women than what was safe and predictable. How would the Joan of Arcs in our midst rise if there was no charge? How would the Maya Angelou's of our generation speak against injustice and tell their stories without a company cheering them on? How would the Esthers and Deborahs move bravely forward if they had no platform to launch from?

The Colour Sisterhood story planted a seed in my heart. A seed that said: *'There is more.'*

The framework and whispers of that moment defined and solidified my YES towards becoming the solution carrier God designed me to be.

'The Lord God said, 'It is not good for the man to be alone. I will make a helper suitable for him.'

12 | YES TO WOMEN

Now the Lord God had formed out of the ground all the wild animals and all the birds in the sky. He brought them to the man to see what he would name them; and whatever the man called each living creature, that was its name. So the man named all the livestock, the birds in the sky and all the wild animals.

But for Adam, no suitable helper was found. So the Lord God caused the man to fall into a deep sleep, and while he was sleeping, he took one of the man's ribs and then closed up the place with flesh. Then the Lord God made a woman from the rib he had taken out of the man, and he brought her to the man.

The man said, "This is now the bone of my bones and flesh of my flesh; she shall be called Woman…"' – Genesis 2:18-23 NKJV

Whenever God makes anything, His response is to pause, gaze upon His created thing, and say: *'It is good.'*

But when He looks at the man alone, tending to the Garden of Eden, working within it, on his own. He responds, *'It is not good for man to be alone.'*

You see, man on his own is an incomplete story. Unfinished to God and unfinished on Earth. A problem needing a divine solution.

How was the man supposed to be fruitful and multiply without a woman? God intended for mankind – man and woman – to govern and lead together.

We know how the story goes. God puts man to sleep; the original Hebrew of the word 'sleep' means 'stunned'. God stuns Adam, creating an *'Ezer Kenegdo'* for him. A solution. A helper. Adam wakes and says she is **'it'.**

In the English language, we've called women helpers, but this does not fully convey the essence of women, the 'Ezer kenegdo'. This attempt to translate Hebrew into English is flawed and has caused many women to feel forgotten, less than and undervalued.

Studying this word and looking at the different root words in its basic translation, it can be better understood as: *'opposite but equal strong partner.'*

For example, my right hand is the *'Ezer Kenegdo'* to my left hand. Both hands look alike, except they are exactly opposite. Both hands are equal but opposite so that they can work better together. Imagine trying to write, dig, or cook with two right hands or two left hands.

The woman is the *'Ezer Kenegdo'* to the man. She is an opposite but equally strong partner put alongside man to subdue the Earth and have dominion. Women bring a necessary completeness and God-breathed solution. We were created to be men's greatest allies.

At the heart of who we are as women is the grand idea that we were created to be a solution. We are solution carriers in this world, equal partners in the Kingdom of God, designed to rule and reign with man.

You are not a problem. You are not an afterthought. You are not second and below. You are not God's backup plan. You are not less than and have certainly not been forgotten.

12 | YES TO WOMEN

You are a strategic and powerful inclusion to this story of humanity. You are valuable. From the beginning, God intended for you to be a 'solution carrier'.

I spent many years believing that my gender made me inferior and disqualified me from living the YES Life. I thought my physiological design disqualified me from being front and centre to all God wants to do on Earth. That my emotional and nurturing nature left me behind. That my fierce feminine heart was a hindrance and an inconvenience. Maybe it's a little too much for people to handle?

If you have ever felt like this, you are not alone.

Sisterhood opened my eyes to the possibility and necessity of a ministry to women within the church. A ministry that carried a new message: a message for a new day. Sisterhood is not something we do to keep women busy and appease their desires. Sisterhood is a strategic God appointment. Heaven knows that when women gather, worship, and are encouraged, equipped and mobilised, all of hell shudders. A purposeful, prayerful woman is petrifying to the devil. He knows women's power to transform their homes, workplaces, neighbourhoods, and nations.

'If you invest in one girl, you're investing in everyone else.' – Melinda Gates.[13]

Gates makes available incredible research highlighting how societies are better when we place value on women. Cities change. Families are more potent, and literacy rates increase. Empathy is introduced at the decision-making levels, and socio-economic climates develop and evolve. Women bring about civilisation. We care deeply and meet human needs. This matters. This should inform us and cause us to sit up and notice.

The Colour Conference gave me the courage and conviction to try something new.
To say YES to a new way of gathering for women.
We must value women and get the men on board to serve the moment.

The template was simple: GATHER – EQUIP – MOBILISE.

We gather. This is our strength.
The Word equips us. This is our empowerment by the Spirit of God.
We are mobilised. This corporate YES urges us to do what God has created us to do in our different spheres of life.

In 2014, we held our first Sisterhood United night in our new Linc Campus auditorium. One hundred and eighty women showed up. I had a sword in my hand, a real-life, heavy-to-hold weapon, and charged us to move bravely forward with a YES to God and a YES to each other.

In 2016, I wanted the Linc Sisterhood to experience the same Colour Conference atmosphere that had stirred me to bring home the Sisterhood dream. Nearly two hundred women from Durban boarded an aeroplane that year. We took over the flight, booked an entire hotel, and blocked out a conference seating block. We arrived with faith, joy, and expectation, and **we did it together**. We were mobilised. We believed in something bigger than ourselves, something bigger for all of us. It was an exciting time, and I will never forget the thrill of the chaos and the buzz of excitement.

Saying YES together has been a signature of the Sisterhood journey and movement. We have always believed in one another, prioritised friendship, and rallied around one purpose and cause. This has had an incredible positive effect on our city.

We've raised money for safe houses.
We've raised money for sanitary wear to keep girls in school.
We've renovated schools.
We've built play centres.
We hosted the first-ever A21 Anti-human trafficking walk in KwaZulu-Natal.
We've got behind the education of children in our city.
We've invested in resources for the Linc Foundation.
We've prayed and believed for breakthrough together.
We've championed a new way for women to interact with one another.
We've placed value upon the men in our world and refused to partner with a narrative that pulls masculinity apart.

We've celebrated the Church. ALWAYS.
Unapologetically, we are first and foremost here to build Her. We've come alongside men to build and establish the Bride of Jesus Christ, the apple of His eye. And it has been the greatest joy being a part of something so spectacular.

I asked God once why he gave me three girls in succession for many years before I had a son. He showed me how He knew that even if

I chose not to pursue my actual value and worth for myself, I would stop at nothing to discover God's heart for my daughters.

Pursuing God's heart for my three young girls has been a wild adventure. As I have pursued His heart for them, the irony is I found His heart for me. I've come to know how much God loves women. His daughters. We are *His* first, and we are most certainly not a problem. The word over us is a big YES from Heaven. We have more options than we realise and carry more solutions and strategies for change than we can ever know. We are a God-ordained strategic part of this story, a gift to the world, bringing completion and wholeness.

What does this story of women and conferences and daughters mean for us all?

It invites us to participate in God's big YES and boldly step into our own YES Life.

When women take hold of their identity, worth, and value, when they believe they are a solution, and when they become determined to be 'that' kind of girl, they become the women God, in His genius, created them to be.

Do you believe you are a solution carrier?
Do you believe that you have something that the world is longing for?
Can you hear the big YES of God over your life?
Can you see it?

God doesn't ask anything of us that He has not already placed within us. You have everything you need to become the woman you were created to be, right from the beginning.

Of course, I cannot write about Sisterhood without exploring the idea of mother. My conviction is firm. Regardless of your ability or inability to conceive, carry, and birth a child, the mother spirit is within every woman.

To be a woman is to carry the heart of a mother, and that looks like
Nurture
Discernment
Clarifying
Mentoring
Leading
Empathy
Strategy
Teaching and training

It looks like showing up at the battlefield.
To say *YES*, even when it is inconvenient or difficult.

Motherhood beckons us all as women towards sacrifice. The spirit of motherhood calls us to shift our thinking. To respond as a mother is to respond as a leader in society. It may start within our homes, but it does not end there. Mothers shape atmospheres and cultures, and the spirit of motherhood is found in every part of our everyday lives.

It is our God-led and God-planned right and responsibility to step up and step into the spirit of motherhood, especially this season when the world is crying out for a mother's comfort, nurture, wisdom and strategy.

Wherever you may be in your life story, whatever phase you find yourself in, I implore you to ask yourself, 'Will I arise as a woman and a mother?'

'What does playing the role of mother in society look like for me?'

You have what it takes within you to make a difference in the world and to become a solution-carrier in our generation. To lead and mentor generations that come after you.

What's holding you back from YES?

13 | YES to Pain

At the beginning of each year, I frame the year with a word. If God's Word and heart over me is one of a big YES, then I have permission to call forth more and more from myself, because I believe that YES calls me to move bravely forward each year.

Words matter, and words are powerful. Words can direct our course and shift our being. Words are a rudder, our true North. Words can shape our worlds and align our behaviour with our desires and beliefs. I am prayerful and considerate in my choice of these 'words'. I like to think and believe that the Holy Spirit whispers these words into my heart. It's incredible to look back at a year and realise how significant and weighty the words have been and how they have directed me along the path I need to take. How they've led me onward and upward in pursuing the life that God has predestined me to live.

In 2019, I spent many hours within the scripture of James 1. I particularly loved the paraphrase that says: *'When it seems as though you are facing nothing but difficulties, see it as an invaluable opportunity to experience the greatest joy that you can! For you know that when your faith is tested, it stirs up in you the power of endurance. And then as your endurance grows even stronger, it will release perfection into every part of your being until there is* **nothing missing and nothing lacking***.'*[14]

The writer asks us to 'consider it all joy when facing trials of every kind.'[15] I became intrigued with the idea of embracing pain rather than numbing it, denying or avoiding it. I saw firsthand how, if I embraced my pain and faced my circumstances, it would leave me better off than before.

I called that particular year the year of 'nothing missing and nothing lacking.' I wanted to bravely face the hard. In hindsight, I am grateful for this YES; however, the process of what I had called into being in real time saw me navigate one of the most consistently uncomfortable years of my life.

In 365 days, I faced years worth of pain buried in the deep recesses of my heart. I guess I had hoped that burying the pain of my past would cause it to disappear. In effect, all I did was stuff it down deep, hoping it would fade over time.

In 2019, I journeyed through some of the pain of my past with a counsellor and did some professional coaching. I faced unspoken trauma. I dislodged resentment and bitterness in my heart. I faced unforgiveness. I tackled my poverty mindset. I faced my overwhelming lack and weakness as a human being. I took responsibility for where I was being deceitful in offering people something that I was not. I owned my inadequacy as a leader and a mentor. I faced these things head-on and allowed myself to embrace the feelings that followed. I had to acknowledge the bitterness, grief, and disappointment in my heart by recognising that there was so much more room to grow, and facing it all was part of this process.

It hurt as I faced my past and my failures. Uncovering the shame was painful, but it was worth it. Any journey through pain has the potential to produce something great on the other side, and over time, I became more healed and perfected. I became more than I imagined I could become.

By saying YES to a 'nothing missing, nothing lacking' narrative and life, and by saying YES to facing my pain, I said YES to crossing over into a new way, a new life. I was choosing God's big YES for me. YES to more. YES to life. I greeted peace, joy, healing, wholeness, and love and bade farewell to the weight of shame, unforgiveness, lack, poverty and failure.

2019 prepared me for the future like I never could have imagined. I didn't know what lay around the corner. I was only responding with a YES to what was in front of me right then, which meant facing all of myself rather than avoiding it for another year.

Levi Lusko says, *'We should train for the trial we are not yet in.'*[16] Without fully knowing it, that is precisely what I was doing when I said YES to pain.

2020 dawned with a global pandemic on the rise, and I was ready for what was coming my way because a year before, I had done hard and holy work. I had faced myself and allowed my heart to acknowledge past mistakes and circumstances that had caused significant pain.

This chapter should not cause you to look for skeletons where none exist. What does saying YES to pain look like? You don't need to look for 'hard' because 'hard' will ultimately find you. And when it does, the best YES you can say is YES to facing it.

I used to run from hard things when I saw them coming, and sometimes, I still do. When I saw discomfort coming my way, I would hide, cover it up, or distract myself, but in 2019, I did something else. I sat in my feelings. Sometimes, I walked alone. Other times, I called for help. I walked through because I knew within the depths of myself that I could no longer afford to avoid my pain. With people's help and being in the Word of God daily, I developed a simple formula that has helped me in uncomfortable spaces of pain and growth.

Look, and then look again. Always look twice.

In James 1, he says to *'see the trials.'*

When confronted with hardship or asked to say YES to life's storms, we can run and hide or face it head-on. The crux of it all is that the only way out is through. Under challenging circumstances and seasons, or when past pain is holding us back, the only way out is through. Going around or walking away from it will only extend the pain. Inevitably, we will have to face it later on.

How do we walk through? We see the trials. We look at the pain. Looking at pain means acknowledging it. We don't pretend it's not there. We don't cover it up. We don't deny it. We feel the feelings. We see that something is out of place and take action.

Recently, I heard a beautiful testimony of a Pastor in America who, before her new life, salvation and role as a Pastor, was a pornographic actress. YES, you just read that correctly. She boldly tells of how she is not ashamed of her story. This fascinated me. How does she do that?

Especially within the church. This is how. She believes that the grace of Jesus Christ, His death and resurrection is so powerful that it removes sin and shame from our lives. And so, if it's gone in His eyes, it's gone in hers. Her conviction is firm, and she has done the hard and holy work to face the pain and shame of her past. She has looked it in the eye and put it in its rightful place. She says Jesus paid the price for her judgement, so she won't live under the criticism and judgement of human beings.

That's saying YES to a 'nothing missing, nothing lacking' kind of life.

Seeing the pain looks like naming it. Seeing the pain means talking through the trauma. Seeing the pain means seeking help. Seeing the pain means acknowledging what could have been in order to move forward.

See it for what it is or was. And then, look again. Look again with hope.

In 2017, my daughter, Honor, fought a superbug infection in the ICU that almost killed her. She experienced trauma and pain, which, in turn, traumatised me. Four years later, I took Honor to see a child psychologist. The psychologist said she doesn't believe Honor is carrying the trauma but feels I may be.

It was a hard moment. Honor was little and vulnerable. It felt wrong and unjust to watch her endure something like that. When I look back, I remember being angry and afraid. I thought she would die. Facing the overwhelming thought that I might lose a child almost destroyed me. I struggled to trust God after that. The ordeal left me fearful and numb.

There were days I believed and felt God and my friends abandoned me. I was lonely. I was unsure. I didn't prepare for it or ask for it. I didn't go looking for the pain – it came looking for me.

To heal and move bravely forward, I had to say YES to dealing with that trauma. To look, and then look again, through a new lens of hope and faith.

I began to heal when I shifted the focus from what I could not understand in my pain to what I knew about God.

That He is good.
That He is faithful.
That He is merciful and gracious.
That He will work all things for the good of those who love Him.
That He never leaves nor forsakes us.
That His grace covers a multitude of sins.
That His mercy meets me in my weakness.
That He is close to the brokenhearted.

Even when we may feel powerless in our circumstances, the beautiful truth is that we are always free to choose. God gives us that. This makes us powerful. We are not powerless in our pain. We can choose the perspective we want to have. It is hard, but we can choose how to respond, and also we can choose the confession we wish to make. We cannot leave this to chance; otherwise, we will cling to the lowest forms of our belief – what we can produce or manufacture in our strength and humanity. In times of trauma and grief, we are not strong. We must

13 | YES TO PAIN

choose a response and confession that is beyond ourselves. We must choose a supernatural confession that strengthens and brings us through.

We can't control the outcomes of circumstances, but we can control our responses. This is not an easy road. It's one fraught with obstacles and grit. It will always ask more of us than we are willing to give. This is, in essence, the reality of the YES road: the road that leads us to the abundant life we all crave and desire.

If 2019 taught me anything, it taught me that how I perceive my circumstances will determine what comes of them.

Nightbirde was a beautiful singer-songwriter who shot to stardom in 2020/2021 after her 'America's Got Talent' audition went viral. Her story speaks straight to the human heart. None of us want to face pain or wade through grief, but we know it's a reality of life. At some point, we will face things we don't want to. Inherently, we all live with bated breath, desperate to know how to grieve and suffer well, how to walk through and cross over.

In a six-minute moment, Jane Marcowski's presence, posture, and words were like balm to our weary hearts during a brutal pandemic. Having fought cancer and confronted another negative diagnosis, Jane shows up and offers her authentic self to the world amidst the pain.

In response to the judges' reaction to her current obstacles and the cancer she is once again fighting, she says, '*It's important that everyone knows that I'm so much more than the bad things that happen to me. You can't wait until life isn't hard anymore before you decide to be happy.*'

THE YES LIFE

Jane had a 2% chance of survival, and yet Jane died. The odds were stacked against her, but her stance of walking within that 2% chance and what she brought to the world amidst it all was like a feast for all the world to enjoy and be inspired by.

She showcased a bold YES and bias towards the 'nothing missing, nothing lacking' way. In response, the world's hearts exploded with admiration and hope. We all found courage in her story to face our challenges and live rebelliously hopeful lives.

Her honest approach to pain gave us hope to fight the battles and endure the storms around us. Her song 'It's Okay' went to number one on the American music charts just a few days after that episode of America's Got Talent aired.

She modelled what it means to look at your circumstances in the face. She looked at her life and looked at it again with a hopeful perspective. She moved bravely forward to the wide-open YES set before her, even though she was months away from her death. I spent many hours wondering how she did it. There is no way of knowing what gave her the strength to write and release songs as she began to die. There seemed to be this defiant hope and willful choosing within her. She was willing to face whatever came her way with grace and faith because this was her one life, and even in its ending, she wanted to be remembered for more than cancer.

Saying YES to a 'nothing missing, nothing lacking' life means choosing to share the burden. A refusal to go alone. As my grandmother reminded me, *'A burden shared is a burden halved.'*

13 | YES TO PAIN

It may seem like a flippant phrase, but a wise truth lies within the knowing that supernatural power can be found in one another. Proud hearts and weary souls can choose to shut people out. But nothing is quite like a friend's shoulder in our most profound valley moments. A comrade. A listening ear. A lover. A carer. The steadiness and empathy of others is crucial to healing.

We must look for those with whom we can share all of life because the ramifications of going alone are tremendous and often add further layers to our pain.

Victor Frankl recalls how life looked grey when he was released from Auschwitz. Beige. Uniform and stagnant. Over time, as he began to share what he had endured, colour began to return to life. Every shade and hue began to find its rightful place within his vision as his heart healed in sharing his trauma.

The Bible's words embrace our hearts when we read that we should 'carry one another's burdens.'[17]

One of the greatest gifts in my life has been friendship. When I feel like the world is spinning off its axis, or the rug has been pulled from under my feet. When my heart hurts or when I have felt bruised, shattered, and scarred. When I am burdened, you can be sure that as I share my whole self with authenticity and vulnerability, as I allow another presence to usher me onward, I feel the pressure dissipate, and the load lighten as others carry it.

We need people in our lives who will listen first and then speak life and truth over us. We don't need people to tell us what we want to hear, but rather the depths of what we truly *need* to hear.

There is no substitute for human connection. There is only so much we can do on our own. If you cannot shift your perspective on your own, you need to surround yourself with people with the perspective you need to make it through. You need to surround yourself with:

People with faith.
People with courage.
People who know how to stand.
People who have weathered their storms.
People who look for the light.
People who carry hope.
People who know how to shift an atmosphere.
People who are not afraid to speak the truth over your doubt.
People who will pull you forward when you can't take another step.
People who will pick you up off the ground and carry you through to the other side.
People who will place the promises of God right at the forefront of your circumstances.

There is a story in the book of Acts about the Apostle Paul being exiled to an island because he won't stop preaching about Jesus. Just before the journey begins, God warns him that the ship will be shipwrecked. He tries to convince the authorities, but they don't listen and set sail anyway. They're quite a way into their journey when a storm picks up.

13 | YES TO PAIN

It's severe, and it's not going to end well. During the storm, the sailors try to abandon the ship, but Paul tells them:

'Friends, you really should have listened to me back in Crete. We could have avoided all this trouble and trial. But there's no need to dwell on that now. From now on, things are looking up! I can assure you that there'll not be a single drowning among us, although I can't say as much for the ship – the ship itself is doomed.

'Last night, God's angel stood at my side, an angel of this God I serve, saying to me, 'Don't give up, Paul. You're going to stand before Caesar yet – and everyone sailing with you is also going to make it.' So, dear friends, take heart. I believe God will do exactly what he told me. But we're going to shipwreck on some island or other.'

'This is the fourteenth day we've gone without food. None of us has felt like eating! But I urge you to eat something now. You'll need strength for the rescue ahead. You're going to come out of this without even a scratch!' – Acts 27: 22-34 MSG

In hard times, we all need a Paul – a friend who will tell us the truth and call us to more. A friend who will help us acknowledge the reality of our circumstances and encourage us through them.

As Paul had warned, the ship did sink, but no one was harmed, and the crew were given a gift through his presence and courage through the storm.

After my miscarriage in 2016, I remember sitting with a friend, feeling hopeless and defeated. The loss engulfed me, and it seemed no one understood. I just couldn't pick myself up. In a raw, beautiful moment, I was embraced by a woman who had suffered many more miscarriages than me and was still fighting a long, painful infertility battle. Her embrace and understanding gave me a gift that night. I felt the affection and care of a woman who acknowledged my pain and could help me see through it.

She shared my burden. She never belittled my pain or asked me to pretend it wasn't there. She didn't try to make it disappear by showing me how much more she had suffered. She reminded me that there was something more significant than what I was experiencing. She transferred the tangible hope I needed to move forward once more.

My heart healed, little by little, as I stood alongside someone who knew the extent of the pain of losing an unborn child. A woman who, within her loss, carried otherworldly trust that I could draw from and find hope in. Her staying solid and true to her story gave me access to what I needed to say YES to face my pain and move bravely forward.

14 | YES to Gratitude

One of the bravest things we can do to face our pain and move bravely forward is to choose gratitude. It is contrary to what we think and know will help our situation. We are not thankful for our pain, but we can find something to be grateful for, even in it.

In 2017, I was weary. The novelty of 'having it all' had worn off. The daily and regular implications of leading, passionately living by example, and loving wholeheartedly as a woman, wife, and mother were tiring me out. With three small children, a full plate of work, and a growing platform, I was living perpetually spent.

I'm not exactly sure why, but I was dissatisfied and frustrated. Something needed to change. I couldn't find joy in places that held great significance and value in my life. The rush of juggling all the different proverbial balls made me anxious, and I couldn't remember why I was 'doing it' any more. *What had I said YES to? Was this the big YES of God over my life, or had I gone off the path somewhere? When was the last time I laughed? Had fun?* Some parts of my painful circumstances were covered and protected by too much activity, and I was caught up in the monotony of getting the job done. I'd slowly moved from a place of 'more than enough' to 'barely getting by'. How had it happened, and what would I do?

On a necessary trip to the Wild Coast to rest and gain clarity, I was given a small book with a picture of a bird's nest on the cover. I was not entirely excited. Seriously? Birds' eggs? It seemed weak and random; however, as I began reading it, the words unlocked something in me, and I cracked my heart open. I slowly thawed, little by little, as bottled-up tears flowed down my cheeks and dropped quietly over my heart and onto my hands.

I shed 1000 tears for the *1000 Gifts* Ann Voskamp gave me in her book. She spoke of pain. She spoke of loss. She told her story. Her heart was opened through pain to see ordinary gifts each day. She found that, within the monotony and discomfort of our daily lives, colourful moments are beckoning for our presence and attention if we just look around.

She noticed and looked for these gifts, wrote them down, expressed them, and then gave thanks. She became addicted to searching for the good, big or small, each day. This led to pages and pages packed to the brim with *1000 gifts*. The little book taught me the art of gratitude.[18]

I was saying YES to living a life marked by gratitude. I partnered with a posture of the heart that inherently knows God is good. God speaks a big YES over our lives. We can always give thanks, regardless of the circumstances around us.

'In everything give thanks; this is God's will for you in Christ Jesus.' – 1 Thessalonians 5:8 NIV

Gratitude has the power to change our lives. Neuroscientists, psychologists, sociologists, and philosophers remind us that thinking grateful thoughts and expressing gratitude contributes to excellent mental, physical, and spiritual health. Gratitude has been known to improve mental well-being and is used as a tool to treat varying degrees of anxiety disorders and depression. We have a muscle in our brains called the pre-congenital anterior circulate: the gratitude muscle. The more it is used, the more it grows. If strengthened over time, this muscle can build a foundation of gratefulness and fortitude within us. These are facts – actual data and science, and according to all this research, grateful people are more successful and have better relationships. So why don't we do it?

An attitude of gratitude can shape how we see the world and influence how we live our lives. It holds the power to move us bravely forward. It's a way of life, a learned behaviour, and a willingness to think differently. An attitude of gratitude is evident when we train ourselves to actively look for the good and then celebrate it.

Gratitude is a perspective that leans towards and embraces all that is worthwhile and positive in the world, even when we don't feel it or believe it. Ann Voskamp says it so beautifully: *'Gratitude takes what we have. And it makes it more than enough. It precedes the miraculous.'*[19]

Gratitude builds within us an abundance mindset based upon what we have and not what we lack. It takes what we have – the real life we have been entrusted with, not the life we wished we had. It takes the raw, the authentic, and the broken and turns it into exceedingly and abundantly more than we could ever imagine.

Gratitude fixes our gaze on what is true, noble, lovely, pure, and holy.[20] When times change, storms rage, and we lose our footing; when our structures of support give way, and when we are still trying to figure out where to turn or what to do, we need something to practice to pull us through. A practice of gratitude, developed over time, will bring us through the difficult seasons of life.

Gratitude is not something reserved for the elite few. It's not a secret that certain special people take hold of. It's a timeless way of living that has produced life and breath throughout the ages, and you can pursue it, too.

In discovering the power of gratitude in my life, I began to listen to and learn from Dr. Caroline Leaf, a neuroscientist. She helps people process information by building healthy thoughts in their brains and is committed to teaching people how to think.

The practice of gratitude starts in our thinking.

Here is a simple formula to get you started on this journey: *Think about what you are thinking about.*

Have you ever considered your thoughts? Where does your mind go? What is the narrative within you? Thinking about what you're thinking about is a powerful way of capturing our thoughts, and it is the starting point for building a habit of gratitude.

The Bible says in Proverbs that *'as a man thinks, so is he.'*[21] That means we become what we think. Our thoughts exist momentarily, but when we agree with them over time, we formulate belief systems that govern our behaviour.[22] Our thoughts are powerful; if we let them run their course, we could end up somewhere we don't want to go. Or, we could go on the most exhilarating adventure of a lifetime.

It's important to deliberately examine what is coming into our minds and pay attention to how we process that information. It's called self-regulation, where we process what's happening in our brains and respond accordingly. Whether we like it or not, our thoughts often pull towards a negative end. We don't instinctively see the good first. When we are conscious about our thinking, we can reframe our thoughts. We can take control and intentionally choose where we want our thinking to end. When I am more present in my thinking, I am empowered to consciously fasten my thoughts to the good.

You may put the book down because you think I am asking you to deny reality. I am not. No good can come from avoidance, denial and suppressed pain. Nothing beneficial flows from toxic positivity. I am asking you to face the reality of your circumstances head-on. Look at it. Acknowledge all the reality. And then, in this place, pull your thoughts towards the good. We do not have to be grateful *for* our pain, loss, disappointment or rejection, but it is possible to be thankful *in* it.

One of the places I find this helpful to do is in my marriage. Perhaps Dylan has forgotten something. He hasn't considered the implications his decisions have on me. He is oblivious to the workload I am carrying. Fill in your marriage stressor blank. Honestly, too often, I have let my thoughts lead me down a rabbit hole of negative thinking about my husband. My immediate annoyance and frustration make it difficult to self-regulate and pull my thoughts towards a positive end. I dwell on the one moment he's let me down, and it takes me to places of prolonged frustration.

When I find myself going down these paths of negativity in my marriage, I am faced with a choice – an opportunity to reframe my thinking. In that moment, I need to stop, think about my thoughts, and acknowledge the good of who he is and all he has done rather than focus on what he lacks.

Yes, Dylan may have let me down. I acknowledge the facts, but refocus my attention on what I know to be true: that his intentions towards me are good. We can not choose to be grateful in a situation unless we consciously think about it.

FEEL A LITTLE

Our feelings build a bridge between our thoughts and choices.

It is crucial to allow ourselves to feel and then connect our thoughts to a feeling so it can be tangible and memorable. Gratefulness makes us feel good inside. It makes us feel whole. It produces joy and peace. It's the feeling that gives that thought tangibility. It gives it an association that causes us to remember.

'Could I write a list of 1000 things? I love to name 1000 Blessings. 1000 gifts. I grab a scrap of paper out of my notebook, and I flip it over. I begin the list, not of the gifts I want, but of the gifts I already have. One morning shatters across the old floors to jam piled high on the toasts, three, the cry of the Blue Jay from high in the spruce. That is the beginning and I smell. I can't believe how I smell; I mean, they just come in things. I don't even know their gifts really until I write them down and that is really what they

look like gifts he did bestow this riding down. It's sort of like unwrapping love writing the list, it makes me feel happy all day. I can hardly believe how it is that I'm swept up in a surging stream of grace and it's wild how it sweeps me away, adding one more to the list of feeling it all again. I am the woman who speaks but one language, the language of full discontentment and self-condemnation, the critical eye, the never satisfied and yet complete, are happy. This makes me giddy almost this list writing of all that is good and pure and beautiful. It makes me feel.[23]

We acknowledge the reality. Then, we must allow ourselves to feel. We present ourselves in that thought and how it makes us feel. This is what allows us to choose how we will respond. To choose to express the good that we see or not.

CHOOSE IT.

It's in our expression of gratitude that something truly begins to shift in our minds and our hearts. It starts with a thought and is strengthened by our feelings. But the power of gratitude to transform who we are lies in the expression of it, and that takes a choice. There is no easy way to do a hard thing.

In 2020, we planned a holiday to Mauritius. The pandemic was looming, but we'd done the homework, and the South African and Mauritian Embassies permitted us to travel. We were safe, or so we thought, and we were excited. Masks weren't a thing, and seven days on an island, given to us as a gift, felt like a dream come true. I was beyond ready for this. I had prayed for and desired it for our family for such a long time. So, we left.

And one glorious beach day later, Mauritius went into total lockdown. The island became deathly quiet, with little or no activity, as people hid indoors. The borders closed. Planes stopped flying. The beaches emptied, and people stayed home. We followed suit, except this wasn't our home. This was a foreign country, and I had come with little to no supplies. We had a church to lead and responsibilities in South Africa. It was a mess. I felt desperate, and I was highly disappointed. Where was God as I consoled the babies on the hour? Where was He as I scanned an open pool constantly because our 2-year-old couldn't yet swim? This was not the plan or the promise. We couldn't access food. Local church island friends were secretly bringing us supplies from their pantries. It was exhausting and stressful.

A few weeks into the lockdown, I had what I now remember as my washing line moment. I was doing the laundry and began to cry as I hung the last set of clothes. I allowed the reality of the moment, the emotion, the pain, the disappointment, the failure to pour out of me. I was angry. It felt unfair and unjust. *'Everyone else gets the best family holidays'*, I cried. I ensured He knew that this was not okay, that I was not OK. I told Him about my sadness and how I felt let down by Him. I shared how hard watching my kids try to understand this strange reality was.

As I calmed down, I heard and felt the gentle whisper I knew all too well. A softly spoken reminder that this was not the end. It was an

14 | YES TO GRATITUDE

encouragement to see that I had been training for this moment for years, and I held *'the way'* in my hand that could strengthen our hearts and homes. I wasn't lost; I knew exactly what to do. I returned from that washing line to the house and promptly called my children to a family meeting. We were going to make a grateful jar and build strength and hope within ourselves as we sat in the unknown circumstances. Every time we felt scared or unsure, we would fill the jar. Little by little. Moment by moment. I did not know what the future held, but I was saying YES to shift the atmosphere in my heart. I chose gratitude for myself and my family.

The shift did come. We didn't leave the island, not for 75 days. But, as we looked for the good, the atmosphere in our beautiful beachside home began to change.

We gave thanks for the hundreds of hermit crabs and that we got to build a hermit crab farm for the first time.
We gave thanks for our beautiful big pool.
We gave thanks for surprise burgers and a pizza treat after ten days of shop closures and minimal food supplies.
We gave thanks for family Zooms and anonymous birthday cake deliveries.
We gave thanks for fresh Pringles and Sprite.
We gave thanks for vanilla rum and the never before tasted strawberry almond white chocolate.
We gave thanks for 75 sunsets. Each one was breathtaking and unique.
We gave thanks in the moment, as scary and uncertain as it was.

We experienced unprecedented generosity and received South African surprises on big days when we needed it most.

We had our online church, and we had Jesus. His kindness and presence in and through it all.

Gratitude caused us to laugh more. We became softer and kinder. We shared stories and made beautiful island friends. We carved out time and made spectacular memories. We beheld the dawn of each new day expectant and hopeful, ready for anything coming our way.

I consciously said YES to gratitude, and in 75 days, I became someone new. I went from crying at the washing line to leaving three months later, crying again because I had fallen in love with the island and its people. I was sad to leave it all behind. I had grown fond of the place and what God was doing on this island. I saw the potential.

Practising gratitude opened my eyes to the reality that was around me.

You cannot conjure that up. You cannot manufacture yourself into a reality. You think about it. You feel it, and then you choose to express gratitude with intention and consistency, no matter what.

As I look back on our time in Mauritius, I realise it was the greatest gift I have ever been given. I learnt so much about myself. I learned to dream differently and courageously entered a new chapter of my life. I faced shame and chose a new way. I embraced uncertainty and saw it as an offering to grow and become. I learned leadership and found a new rhythm and pace. I found the whispers of Heaven in the still, sweet midnight moon moments and discovered that the exchange of beauty for ashes is accurate and true.

Mauritius is what gave me my season of 'Tea with Tes'. A weekly community of women who knew how to pray and show up for one another. A platform that allowed me to grow in influence and has sharpened my prophetic gift and teaching ability. I will forever be grateful for this unlikely start and the thousands of women who have been part of it, all because of a simple YES.

Miracles happen on the other side of saying YES to gratitude. A million little miracles. Grace gifts flow towards us daily when we think, feel, and then choose to see the good.

15 | YES to Giving It All Away

Have you ever found yourself in places of deep questioning?

It's great to ask questions, but it can be tricky when you start looking for the answers in all the places surrounding your life. Extracting what you need from anyone and anything who will give it to you can be dangerous and cause you to be whipped about by the wind and waves.

The Covid pandemic lured me into this place of deep questioning, and then losing my dad so suddenly provoked more and more questions. Difficult circumstances called me to sit and reevaluate my life from a new perspective. How I was living challenged me, and grief poked at so much of my life. It brought things out of hiding that were holding me captive from living the kind of life that would be remembered and celebrated.

I began to rediscover myself. I said YES to figuring out who I am. I asked God to eliminate shame from every part of my life and help me grow and evolve as a woman. I was willing to try new things and show up with courage. I wanted to live fully alive in my God-given purpose, even if I wasn't entirely sure of what that was. I wanted to deal with my fear of man. It was time to put myself out there, even if I failed dismally.

Who is Tes? I asked again and again. When the lights are off, and the social media is packed away? When the crowd is gone, and I sit with myself? Who am I?

What matters most?

Only once we know who we are and what we value can we choose to give it away.

Saying YES to being me was brave, and every brave YES I said awakened something more.

It awakened me to my God-given gifting and anointing.
It awakened me to lead.
It awakened me to speak.
It awakened me to write.
It awakened me to sing.
It awakened me to my strategic thinking.
It awakened me to the extent of my creativity.

I know who I am, which has given me the confidence to say an even bigger YES. I can put myself out there and engage in intimidating environments. What I have to offer is needed. I am not trying to prove anything anymore. I tell myself almost every day, *'you belong in the rooms you are invited to, Tes.'*

I framed another year, 2021, with my YES to givenness – YES to give away my best every single day. Now that I knew who I was and what I held, the best YES I could say was YES to give it away.

With this new year and new word came the invitation to walk towards what I call 'the given life'. I knew God was asking me for more than just self-discovery and self-awareness. I knew there was an uncovering of more extraordinary things in Him, and I began to see how a purposeful life was a 'given life'.

At the heart of it all, I never wanted to be stuck in the place of just figuring out my gifts and talents for the sake of just knowing. I wanted to take a risk, own what I saw and what was clearly affirmed by great people around me, and then just give it away. Every. Single. Day. I didn't want to be remembered as someone who held on so tightly to my God-given gift that no one else benefited from it.

Saying YES to a given life that is not predominantly for me but for future generations means saying YES to showing up with my purpose.

'The question that drives our lives needs then to be: How do I now give my life away more generously and purely? How do I do this better? Living for something beyond ourselves is what is being asked of us during all these years. But we are rarely ready. It is comforting to know we need only be willing... We move beyond the cancer of frustration and restlessness by precisely accepting that here, in this life, there is no finished symphony. We carry the infinite inside ourselves. We are Grand Canyons without a bottom. Nothing, short of union with all that is, can ever fill that void. To be tormented by complexity and restlessness is to be human. To make our peace with that is to come to peace, and we are mature to the degree that our restlessness is no longer the centre of our lives.' – Ronald Rolheiser[24]

Givenness is less about us, and more about building generationally, than we realise. It's a choice to see the gifts, know the resources we hold in our hands, and be willing to give it all away.

To give, and give again, because we know God is writing a big YES story that is infinite and inclusive.

'As each of you has received a gift (a particular spiritual talent, a gracious divine endowment), employ it for one another as [befits] good trustees of God's many-sided grace [faithful stewards of the extremely diverse powers and gifts granted to Christians by unmerited favour].' – 1 Peter 4:10 AMP

To employ means to make available. Now that I know what I hold within me, my signature God-given gift to the world, my next step is to make it available. *Would I say YES to a life that consistently gives myself away as a holy sacrifice? Could I?*

I had this nagging concern about living 'spent'. I needed to figure out how to live within the tension of givenness and real-time exhaustion. In the seasons where I have felt spent from my daily showing up, I have always returned to the wise words of a friend and coach. He has often reminded me that showing up as yourself matters the most. We cannot consistently operate at our best 10/10. Some days, we are 3/10. Other days, we are 5/10 or 7/10. No matter where we are, we can show up at our best, which can look like my best 3/10 self. Saying YES to the given life means making peace with showing up at 3/10. I may be at 3/10, but I can still bring my best 3/10 to the table and add value. I can still freely give all of myself because it is what I have been entrusted with – not for myself, but for others.

Givenness is wildly inconvenient. But solution carriers and YES-sayers embrace the inconvenience because they know that they must let go of their agendas for big things to happen. We need to allow our lives to

15 | YES TO GIVING IT ALL AWAY

be interrupted and disrupted by the notion that we are part of a bigger plan. It's more than just about me. We're invited to give ourselves away for something divine.

'Truly, truly, I tell you, whoever believes in Me will also do the work that I am doing. He will do even greater things than these, because I am going to the Father.'[25]

Jesus did all the hard work and all the heavy lifting. He set it all up, gave all of Himself away, and then invited us to respond the same. It is then up to us to reply with a YES and move bravely forward, further, and higher than ever before.

For lasting supernatural change to take place, it will take passionate, relentless people who will stop at nothing. It's going to take a given person – a surrendered people – men and women who will choose to say YES despite the inconvenience.

Kathryn Kuhlman, an American preacher in the 1950s famous for healing crusades and preaching, was asked what it cost her to be who she was. She responded by saying:
'Everything, darling. SIMPLY everything.'

Being a given person. It will cost you something. It may cost you everything. Do not be afraid of the cost. It's okay to live a life spent for the sake of Jesus and the call He has for your life. We tend to play it safe. We live in a convenience-driven generation. We retreat the moment it doesn't meet the criteria of what we think we are capable of. We're so focused on building our empires and agendas that we miss out on His glorious adventure. We miss out on what awaits those who wholeheartedly embrace YES.

I am the first to say I don't always get this right. I like my plans. I enjoy the familiar. I once dreamt of living a white picket fence life with a husband, two kids and a dog. I also get tired. I have hidden behind screens, and still sometimes take extended toilet breaks to find breath and courage for what is required of me. I've wanted to quit more than once. I have wanted to give up.

Let's agree. This God-breathed life is hard. But here's the thing: holding ourselves back is more challenging, and if not now, it definitely will be down the line. Nothing great ever came from the easy road. Those who choose to walk the narrow road will receive life.[26] I'm crazy enough to believe that the world will change when we embrace inconvenience and choose to say YES to givenness. To give it all away, whatever we hold within ourselves, so that people in our world would come alive.

Even now, there are days I feel exhausted. Life is full. Sometimes, it's so full that my arms are aching, and my head is spinning with the reality of all I am being asked to steward. And yet, again and again, I hear the gentle whisper in my heart to give it all away.

The invitation of the given life is to decide in my heart that the answer is YES. YES and YES. No matter what, God, before you ask, the posture of my heart is YES. I am no longer afraid of what obedience will cost me because I have always been given something precious, pure, holy, and sacred in return. He's given me Himself and His presence each time I have given myself away. What more could I ask for?

16 | YES in the Middle of the Night

The days were long. Each night, Paul slept wherever he could find space. The opportunities to tell people about this message of Jesus and this new way of believing and living were growing daily. The invitations to go to foreign people and uncharted places were coming furiously towards him. People were fascinated by what this fearless apostle had to say. Their group was growing, and there were complex dynamics to navigate as Jews and Gentiles found ways to engage in a new way together.

This particular night, he felt spent, wrestling with the knowledge that he was being kept from Asia, the place he longed to go. A place crying out for this gospel message to ignite the Spirit's flame in people's lives.

It was in the middle of the night that he had a vision. His mind was blurry with sleep, yet he saw a man from Macedonia. He was taller than average and had distinctive creamy skin – skin that gave away his ethnicity and deep-rooted history. Like many from Europe, his eyes were like pools of honey with green flecks sparkling around the edges. This man was not just a dream but a vivid reality. He was crying out in desperation, asking Paul to listen.

His words haunted Paul's mind and arrested his heart.
'Come. Please come. Come to Macedonia.'

The picture was clear. Paul knew this was not something random but rather a clarion call to change the plan and move away from Asia towards Europe.

With a swift urgency, Paul immediately gathered his followers and headed for Macedonia. They had no idea what was waiting there, but God did. Paul was convinced of this, so he responded faithfully and quickly, with an obedient heart. He had settled that God was beckoning him towards an open door. Paul believed that Macedonia was crying out for the gospel of Jesus to be preached. Paul said YES to Macedonia and trusted God to lead the way.[27]

This story is a small piece of scripture nestled within the groundbreaking stories in the Book of Acts. It's almost easy to miss as we get caught up in the miracles and wonders of a tenacious group of people who had discovered Jesus. But it's there: a simple story with profound truth for today. The time Paul said YES in the middle of the night.

Often, my invitations to say YES have come in the night. Even as a person who doesn't feel they need much sleep, I still don't enjoy being woken up. I feel disoriented and unsure when I'm awakened from a deep sleep. I struggle to make sense of where I am and what is happening. But I know God wakes me to get my attention when I am quiet and vulnerable.

I believe God often asks us to say YES in the middle of the night. In the middle of the night, we are at our most unfiltered, less guarded and prepared, less likely to overthink, and more inclined to respond as our most authentic selves.

16 | YES IN THE MIDDLE OF THE NIGHT

This book was a YES in the middle of the night. A call and a picture as I fought my dark night of a COVID pandemic and what that meant for my daily schedule.

'I am busy. Let me quantify that, because we are all busy. My life is uncomfortably and frantically full. It's fast-paced, and there is constant movement from one thing to the next thing to the next thing. I run, and then I am running. Constantly juggling. Dropping all the balls. I am failing miserably at my attempts to love my husband, be his friend, mother my kids, school my girls, navigate the one still at school with homework and extras, throw a ball to Joel and stimulate his bright mind, feed them good food, lead the church, work for the church, build new strategies and systems, pastor people and be a good daughter, sister, and friend. Feed the dog, walk the dog. Am I bored? Am I restless? Or am I just exhausted? This doesn't feel like a book season. It doesn't make sense on paper. There is no time. I have no margin. I have no breathing room.' – Journal entry 2021

On a random Tuesday in 2021, I saw an advert for a 'Write Your book' course on my Instagram feed. I felt a nudge. I heard the whisper and knew God was inviting me to say YES. This was an opportunity to look back, heal, and make a bold effect with my words, because the written word is forever. This was an invitation to try something and perhaps even fail. It was a call to step up and into something unknown.

It felt impossible to me. I would need His Grace, rely desperately on the Holy Spirit to pull this off, dig deep and pull from my community, find the support and presence of my husband, put aside self-sufficiency and performance, and say YES to the process. I was afraid of putting my story out there, but it was exhilarating to say YES once more… in the middle of the night.

I love the story of Paul's call to Macedonia. It reminds all of us of the power of vision. If we don't have a vision or picture of what could be, alongside the conviction that it should be, we don't have anything to say YES to.[28]

Vision gives way to life. When a clear picture of something is being laid before us, we can offer our best YES in response.

Proverbs 29:18 has always remained a true North for me. It says, *'Without vision, people perish.'*[29]

Where there is no vision, things die. When there is no vision, our 'no' leads the way. A YES to a bold vision must call us forward. To say YES, we must see the vision.

For many years, I felt I had little vision. I would often feel uncertain about what exactly it was God was asking me to do. I would wrestle with myself, trying to figure out the perfect and best YES to say. I was afraid of making the wrong choices. I didn't want to miss God. I wanted everything He had for me, and in my efforts to control the outcomes, I often got stuck, unable to move forward in faith towards all the things He was inviting me into. At some point, I decided to attach myself to a vision beyond me. A vision that was not my own. Something bigger than my own story. A vision that made my heart leap and called me towards the YES Life of more.

16 | YES IN THE MIDDLE OF THE NIGHT

This vision belonged to Dylan. When I couldn't make out what was being asked of me, the easiest and most natural thing to do was to align myself with something inspiring and grand, to serve and submit myself to something bigger. To take hold of hope, so my faith could take hold of the big YES Life.

I stumbled upon something beautiful in this. As I got up each day and said YES to help Dylan realise the preferred future he saw so vividly, I began to see and visualise a bigger vision for my life. My imagination was awakened to all of the possibilities. The reality of a life pregnant with God-inspired purpose and plans was suddenly more alive in me. I began to see open-door invitations to say YES all around me.

With a renewed sense of vision and a heightened ability to see the YES invitations being presented, I realised that what I saw for my life fit so well with where God was taking Dylan. It was meant to be all along. I just didn't know where or how to look for it.

Aligning yourself with a vision more significant than your own is one of the greatest ways to unlock grace and favour. When we're brave enough to admit that we don't know and then choose to follow somebody else, we can move towards the 'more' God has for us, even when it isn't our own.

Humility is a powerful thing. It moves us out of the way and ushers in God's grace. It takes our little and gives us more than we could dream of, leading us towards a big YES Life.

Paul was utterly uncomplicated. He was asleep. He saw a vision and decided it was God. So, he gathered his followers and redirected their mission to Macedonia, the gateway to Europe.

There is immense power in a quick-footed response. YES, consider it, weigh up all the options, ask for good counsel, and consider the costs. *Then do something. Be immediate.*

Lean towards YES. Walk towards that dream or response or invitation. Take the step. Move bravely forward towards a grander vision, even if it's not your own.

The best kind of obedience is quick obedience.

I have grown to trust the gentle whispers that find their way into my heart – the nagging nudges toward things that often seem crazy and wildly inconvenient. Most times, they are God calling me toward something that will be good for me and good for many.

A long time ago, I rejected 'the big, loud, booming voice from the sky' mentality. I don't believe God speaks like that. I stopped looking for smoke signals. I've grown braver and more efficient in asking God what He wants and waiting patiently for a response. If I don't hear or receive an impression, I act with my God-given brain and just make a decision that is true to Him, His call over my life and the values He has placed in my heart.

In the past, I have often done nothing out of the fear that I could get it wrong. Nowadays, I choose something, knowing that I can trust God to fill in the gaps or redirect me if I go off course. I am more intent on saying YES and moving bravely forward than 'getting it right.' A quick YES is always more powerful than a complex 'maybe'. We can wrestle these options out. We can deliberate, and sometimes we should, but not forever. A bold and quick YES catalyses remarkable stories in history where people have done extraordinary things. There will be questioning, and there will be doubt. There will be moments when you may feel afraid or uncertain. Your YES will cost you something. Your YES will likely be inconvenient. Say YES anyway.

Paul's YES all those years ago is significant. He paved the way for many others, like you and me, to say a brave YES, too. His YES led him to Lydia from the colony in Philippi, a place within Macedonia. That YES changed the course of church history in Europe and ultimately changed the trajectory of my life, too.

Lydia is the first known and recorded conversion to Christianity in Europe. She was a wonderful woman who used her feminine genius to spread the word about a man called Jesus. Her YES gave life and breath to what is known today as the church in Philippi spoken of in the Bible. A church that has inspired and given life and context to our Linc Church community that we birthed on the North Coast almost 16 years ago.

17 | Do it Afraid

'Sometimes fear does not subside, and one must choose to do it anyway.' – Elisabeth Elliot

I had said YES to this book, but so much of me wanted to take this YES back. I knew that nothing with God ever entirely made sense. More often than not, He invites us into the impossible. He asks us to give Him room to do something miraculous with our YES. I said YES, knowing all of this. Then, it got tricky. As I tried to share myself between all my responsibilities, I realised that there was every realistic possibility that I would not finish. I would fail. I would fail as a creative thinker. I would fail as a writer. I would fail at stepping out. I would fail at telling my story. I would fail at trying something new. I would fail at saying YES.

I was afraid.

I wasn't afraid of telling my story or of the process of discovering the author within me. I was scared of the idea of failing. I still am. I felt so stirred to do this but didn't want to fail. I wanted to be brilliant. I needed to achieve this. Now, I was facing the possibility of not finishing.

The 'five years ago Tes' would have said YES to do something scary and out of her depth, but she would have done it secretly, lowering the possibility of failure. She would have eliminated the areas of risk so that if she failed, she could write it off as a bad idea and nurse her wounds in silence. Nobody would know.

The problem was that I wasn't that girl anymore. I had publicly expressed my YES and called out YES in others. Why did I do this? Because it was worth it.

I have gone on a beautiful and painful journey of self-discovery. It's been a tremendous growth journey, facing myself and understanding how I am wired. The 'why' behind Tes helped me recognise why I respond like I do. When I looked at the internal dialogue in my mind, I identified that I was afraid to fail and owned it. Only then could I peel back the layers and ask myself: What was so scary about failing? What was so bad about not finishing this book anyway?

In this process, I became aware that failure was not what was paralysing me. It was shame. Shame shouted over my life that I was not enough and did not have what it took to do something like this. I was afraid of not finishing – not because of failing something – but because I didn't want to feel ashamed because of what others would say or think.

Shame is ruthless. Shame holds the power to shape the way we think and behave. Shame has the crippling ability to render us powerless. Shame may be a buzzword we all know, but it's something that no one wants to face.

Brene Brown says it brilliantly:
'Shame is the master emotion that causes us to fear that we are not good enough.'[30]

17 | DO IT AFRAID

It would have been easier to tell no one. If I didn't finish or it wasn't well received, I would not feel ashamed. Uncovering shame is painful and brutal. I don't want to disappoint myself or others, and I don't like to feel like I am not enough.

Writing this book has revealed how much I still have to grow and become.
I am afraid of getting hurt. And yet, here I am.
I am afraid of showing the world the essence of who Tes is. And yet, I show up.
I fear rejection once I put myself out there, yet so much is already 'out there'.

'Real courage is when you know you're licked before you begin, but you begin anyway and see it through no matter what.' – To Kill a Mockingbird[31]

Of all the people I know who have overcome fear to say YES, no story like Queen Esther has gripped my heart and helped me move bravely forward.

Esther had been groomed and fashioned for years because she was not one of them; she had taken every opportunity to learn and become so that she would be enough for him. The King. Nothing in her wanted to be here. This was not her home. Everything she knew had been violently snatched from her when the King's men had forced her into this pageantry. Esther desperately needed the King to see her because she would not reconcile herself to the fate of a forgotten concubine. And so, she arrived each day present, willing and humble. She prayed and worked. She was promoted and identified as a treasure. Before Esther knew it, the decision to move forward and say YES, despite her fear, paid off.

Esther was now Queen. No longer Haddasah, relative of Mordecai, but Queen Esther of Xerxes, the one the King had chosen.

The King's affection for her was growing. With each moment spent with him, her favour increased. There were moments when she even felt cherished by this foreign man. She had captivated his attention and heart with her flawlessness and exemplary way. Esther became more than just the title of Queen. She became his friend.

Then, things changed. Fuelled by greed and power, a man named Haman, advisor to the King, began to plot against the Jewish people because of his hatred for Mordecai.

In a fateful twist of events, this man, with expert manipulation and skill, gets the King to order the destruction of the Jews in a matter of days. As a Jewish woman who had seen the brutality and injustice of her people before, Esther had to face the enormity of this decree. She was safe within the confines of the royal palace, but what of her people? Could she stand by and watch this unfold? What would she do, and how would she do it?

She could not walk into the King's quarters unannounced. Esther had to wait to be called, to be wanted, to be needed, and to be heard. Her people's fate hung in the balance of his seeking her out and requesting her presence. He wasn't calling for her, and the days kept passing as the awful fate of the Jewish people in Persia was imminent. To show up in his space was to assume death. It was to invite him to end her life out of disobedience and dishonour. There were no guarantees. He may not raise his sceptre. He may not usher her in. He may not beckon her forward. Was she willing to face death at the expense of her people?

In anguish, Esther ran to the man who raised her, who taught her about a God who fights for His people and had shaped the inherent knowing of what was right within her. As they spoke and prayed together one last time, he implored her to do something daringly courageous. Mordecai urges her to go to the King and cry out for justice. He whispers into the terrified parts of her heart that her position and life story were not by chance. She was not in her position because of her own doing. It was not because of her upbringing. It was not by right. She was where she was because this was the moment for which she was created. He ends their moment together by calling her towards her destiny and deposits within her the possibility that she was 'born for such a time as this.'[32]

The plot thickened as she set her face like a flint towards the King. She would go to him and reveal Haman's evil schemes. She would show him Haman had used him to destroy an entire nation. She would do it, even if she died in the process.

Esther entered the King's presence outside of his call. He lifted his sceptre and invited her in. With her brilliant and strategic mind, Esther asked for his presence at a banquet and invited Haman to attend, too.

It is not long before Haman's betrayal and schemes are revealed, and the King reverses the decree he was tricked into signing. Haman is publicly executed, and Esther, along with all of her people, is saved.

This story has become a much-loved narrative for the nation of Israel and women everywhere. The account of one woman's YES in the face of significant opposition and perhaps even her death.

I often try to place myself in her shoes. Scholars say she would have been in her late teens and early twenties. Esther was thrust out of her safe and simple existence and forced to fit a cultural norm that was not her own. She was commissioned to a royal, somewhat lonely life. She then has to face her people's lawful and yet unjust possible extermination. Through all of this is the realisation. She's the one. She is it. Esther was the only one with the power and access to change the King's mind and save her people.

She must have been terrified, yet despite her fear, she says YES. Esther steps forward and takes action. She doesn't wait for the feeling of fear to disappear; she steps forward amidst all she feels. This is what makes all the difference.

Fear is a strange thing. We hate how it makes us feel and act, yet we hold tightly to it, hoping to find relief in our firm grip. Fear doesn't go away when we ignore it or deny it. Fear doesn't shrink when we grab hold of it and keep staring at it. Fear loses its power when we face it and move bravely forward despite it.

I love how Steven Furtick says:
'Faith doesn't take the fear away; it gives us the strength to fight it.'[33]

If we wait until we aren't afraid, we will never do anything. We'll become stuck in our wish to be fear-free. The bravest thing we can do is embrace faith and do whatever it is, despite fear, say YES, afraid.

One of the most courageous things I've done year after year is deal with my heart and the shame that threatens to keep me in hiding. I've shown up when I've wanted to hide. I've faced my weakness and ugly parts. I've acknowledged my pain and the pain I may have caused others. I've spoken about my past and my failures. I've apologised more. I've recognised my poor efforts at leadership. I've humbled myself to receive feedback. I've acknowledged that to some I am a disappointment. I've embraced my story and the faith freely given to me to live out my life every day. It's been costly at times, but well worth the cost.

As I've continued this writing journey, I have seen how distorted my fear of failure is in terms of what others think. Will they like this? Is it worth publishing? Who could learn anything from my life? What if I'm not really a writer? These internal conversations are honest, but they can take me to confusing places within myself if left unattended. I have had to repeatedly stop these thoughts in their tracks.

I have made peace with the fact that everyone will always have an opinion. People will have opinions about this book. We live in a world that places great value on what others think. We don't want to care so much, but hold people's opinions dearly. It matters. Sometimes, even those closest to us don't know how their opinions hold us back. Saying YES in these circumstances is very difficult. It requires conviction and outrageous faith to live beyond what others think and say.

I shared the story of our lockdown in Mauritius earlier in this book. There were many precious God-gifted days that I will treasure forever, but there were also days when I felt paralysed by fear.

I felt stirred to rise and be something, but I was surrounded by four sweet babies who didn't quite understand what was happening. My husband was carrying so much on his shoulders, and the critics and naysayers seemed so loud in my ears. We sensed that God was calling us to use what was in our hands, asking us to lead and influence while shutting down.

I was terrified. Leading from paradise island? What would people say about that?

Again, I stood by that creaky washing line, and I felt the courage of Heaven fill my heart. This was not the time to shrink back and say no to the call to stand as people buckled around us. This was a grand opportunity to say YES to God once more. I felt Him remind me that this was the moment for which I was born. I had been training for this all along. He had been grooming me. Preparing me. Readying me for this very time in history. I couldn't wait to 'feel' strong and ready to face it all. I could do it, afraid.

How do we access courage in these moments? What do we do when we can't find the encouragement we need from the people around us? We learn to find strength and courage from the only One who can give us exactly what we need.

King David knew how to find courage outside of his ability. In his darkest moments, he learnt the practice of encouraging himself in who God is.[34] The word 'encourage' means 'to fasten oneself to courage, establish or fortify, and persuade through support'. Learning to encourage yourself by fastening yourself to the ultimate example of courage is one of the most important things you can learn to do.

Allowing the Holy Spirit to train us in self-encouragement will give us confidence, establish our faith, and fortify our minds.

In Mauritius, I simply did what I knew to do. I practised self-encouragement, and I gave myself daily pep talks. I reminded myself of the truth I knew, even though my feelings were overwhelming. I spoke the words I knew I needed and didn't rely on the opinions I heard or the news that was causing my heart to race. I began to sing a new song over my situation and I accessed the courage already within me for this moment. As believers, we have Christ in us; this is where we find our inner strength and courage.[35]

I said YES to whatever was next and whatever God asked as my courage grew daily on that island. In those three months, I grew more as a leader with an iPhone in my hands than ever before.

18 | Words Matter

Words don't just matter. Words are everything.

'Words attract presence, and you and I determine what kind of presence we want to attract. Sometimes we create land mines to our destiny through our own words.' – Bill Johnson

With one small word or sentence, we hold the power to create or destroy life around us. YES is a powerful word. YES bursts through an open door or walks away from it. YES holds power to move us bravely forward, or we can use it to distract ourselves from the bold life that awaits us.

If you lived in our home for a week, you would hear, 'Think about your words' every day. My greatest endeavour is guiding my children to be conscious of their words. I believe that training them in the ways of God means shaping their language and inner narrative.

Solomon hands us wisdom when he says that *'death and life lie in the power of the tongue.'*[36] Our tongues are like rudders on a boat. All too often, we allow them to steer us in a direction we don't want to follow and, in doing so, fail to create life-giving spaces around us. The YES Life demands that your words hold within them a curve towards what is possible rather than what is not.

Dylan once said, 'Words create worlds.' If you read the beautiful Creation poem in Genesis, you will see that spoken words created the Earth in its shape and form. 'Let there be…' and there was. God uses His life, breath and words to create a world He dreamt of. With every 'Let there be…' came an expression of God Himself here on Earth. Genius. Brilliance. Creativity.

His words gave life. The same reality applies to the words we use today. The same creative potential God uses to create our existence is within us and found within our words. Our words give us the power to create once more. God's 'Let there be' shows what is possible when we say YES.

Have you ever heard that statement, *'Out of the heart, the mouth speaks'*?[37] We don't fully realise the influence we hold to shape something around us based on what we believe. If we paid attention to what we contribute with our words, we would be shocked at what is in our hearts.

There was a moment when I intentionally changed my narrative. I knew God was asking me to shift my language. I could see a YES Life, but my words were not following. My natural tendency was just to say whatever I thought or felt. I was so proud of how 'real' I was, but 'my truth' was standing in direct opposition to His.

I needed help. No matter how hard I tried, I kept tearing down people and things around me with words. I was living the analogy I teach my kids, where you squeeze all the toothpaste out of the tube and ask them to try and get it all back in. We can't take our words back. Once your words have been spoken, they are spoken.

18 | WORDS MATTER

As I tried to work this out, a good friend encouraged me to 'think about what I was thinking about.' She was confident that if I could become conscious of my thinking, I would find the ability within me to speak more intentionally. I could pull my thoughts to higher ground, which would, in turn, allow my words to follow.

Thinking about our thoughts is an effective coaching tool. It helps us define our values, beliefs, responses, and choices. It's a great way of becoming more present in our lives. This practice is challenging for me. My thoughts are pretty raw and unfiltered, and I shudder to think of others getting inside my head. Analysing my thoughts, I realised I had an unhealthy thought process around myself, which ultimately transferred itself onto others.

The brutal truth is that what lurks on the innermost inside parts of us will, eventually, come out. I soon realised that my poor self-esteem was ruling my inner world. I was holding myself captive because of comparison and insecurity. Being present in my thoughts and working through them helped me change my language and tell a new story. I partnered with the narrative of Heaven. This practice enabled me to bring forth the words that create life-giving worlds. The language of life, courage, kindness, and hope.

In his second letter to the Corinthians, Paul encourages us to *'take captive our thoughts'*.[38] Arresting our thoughts is crucial. There is a world waiting to be created with our words. A world crying out for our YES words that will shape the world in which we live. A world longing for words that echo the God of a big YES and a small no. Our world waits for the YES that resounds with Good News, where hope and faith are alive. Where gratitude bridges the gap towards wholeness and contentment, and where courage is accessed. The time for YES to shape our words and world is now.

Pastor Ray Bevan says: *'His Word in my mouth is as powerful as His Word in His mouth.'*
Let's get His Word in our mouths.

I don't know your situation; however, wherever we find ourselves – this is the crux of the story. We choose our response, our words.

'As high as the Heavens are above the Earth,
So, my ways and my thoughts are higher than yours.
As the snow and rain that fall from Heaven
do not return until they have accomplished their purpose,
soaking the Earth and causing it to sprout with new life,
providing seed to sow and bread to eat.
So also will be the word that I speak;
it does not return to me unfulfilled.
My word performs my purpose and fulfils the mission I sent it out to accomplish.' – Isaiah 55:8-11 TPT

Words carry weight. When we carelessly throw words out there, we cannot take them back. A YES Life demands that words of life go before any behaviour or action. This will shape how we show up.

When I look back at my life, I want to be able to confidently say that I used my words to shape an atmosphere of hope, faith, and kindness.

18 | WORDS MATTER

I want to say I wholeheartedly used my life for a big YES that shouted loud over humanity.

His word over me is YES. Therefore, YES can and will shape my words, too.

19 | What is the YES Life?

A year ago, I sat in a room full of big people to celebrate forty years of faithful church-building. Some were large in stature, but all had one thing in common: they were just ordinary people who said an extraordinary YES.

I listened to their stories of how one YES catalysed another and how lives were forever changed. Men and women moved continents, prayed, started churches, sacrificed time with their families, and gave up careers – all on a word from God. None of it made sense, yet they acted.

The story goes that one man and woman who loved to surf and their five-year plan said YES to establishing a wild Jesus-following church in the city of Durban. Their YES attracted many more young men and women to join them, and they, too, would say YES to the adventure of a lifetime.

A young man with broad shoulders and a big personality trying to figure out a life-threatening diagnosis walked through the doors of this wild church. With broken dreams and an uncertain future, he encountered courage and felt stirred to say YES to ministry and a life devoted to the church.

The couple where it began said YES again. They felt the whisper to go to America and passed on the baton of leadership to the young man who encountered Jesus in his broken, uncertain state.

Many more people left the shores of Durban, year after year, each of them obediently following God's lead and calling to go. One such couple said YES to build a church within the landscape of Pretoria, choosing the veld over their love for the sea.

Marriages, children, and many a YES later, this tented church is handed to the young man, with dreams restored, who stepped up to lead the church in the wild on the shores of Durban. Still convinced of his calling, he again says YES to a new season with his family – a new climate, a new day, and a fresh conviction.

Fast forward a decade, and here I sit. It's 2023, and I'm positioned in this grand picture of grace surrounded by all these interwoven YES stories. Where one YES Life called forth the next, and a brave move forward supernaturally stirs someone else's heart. One YES is a contagious invitation for another, and I get to witness what it looks like to live 65 years of radical obedience. Obedience that is formed and fashioned by the One who goes before and paves the way for all of us to say a bold YES to a big God story. To say YES to move bravely forward.

Listening to their stories and testimonies of God's faithfulness got me thinking about my endeavour to live the YES Life – to live with a spirit of YES deeply embedded within my soul. A conviction that it is always better to lean towards YES and live without hesitation when the urge for YES arrives.

19 | WHAT IS THE YES LIFE?

I have this strange thing I do. Because let's say it like it is—-the YES Life is hard. It often doesn't make sense. Every time I overcome how unsure and afraid I am with my YES, I stand in a location of beauty and significance, with my heart towards Heaven and my hands lifted high, and I take a picture. I call it my YES picture. It speaks of openness and surrender. It is a stance of radical, obedient humility and defiant victory. I capture these images to remind myself that this YES was worth saying. It may be hard, but I know I can do hard and holy things. I can make courageous choices and move bravely forward. I've done it before, and I will do it again.

YES has a posture. Straight back. Hands high. Heart open. Eyes lifted to heaven. A stance that says here I am, I will go.

The YES Life lives beyond what we can control and confine. It demands that I put my wholehearted trust in God, who sees the bigger picture when I can't. He is the One who can see what is coming around the corner. The YES Life lives beyond a white picket fence dream and beckons us to walk the path less travelled. The YES Life is a narrow road where one YES leads you bravely forward, one step after another.

It may feel uncomfortable at times. It may cause you to walk straighter and slower. It may ask you to think critically about the placement of your feet. When you feel this way, do not run from the discomfort of the narrow road.

Jesus Himself talks about the narrow road that leads to LIFE.[39] What life? Resurrected Life. His way is indeed the core of this YES Life, a YES He walked towards. A narrow road paved for Him that would ultimately lead Him to His death – the same road that made the way for us to say YES with conviction and confidence today.

We do not go alone, but rather, walk alongside the One who knows firsthand the cost of YES and who says it anyway. YES, despite the whole plan. YES, without the assurance of safety. YES, with great pain. YES, knowing you may lose everything to gain everything.

Saying YES could give you the relationships you always dreamed of.
Saying YES could usher in a new day in your life.
Saying YES could give you the family you always wanted.
Saying YES could remove you from toxicity and abuse.
Saying YES could land you in rehab with help.
Saying YES could surround you with people who put courage in your soul.
Saying YES could lead you to a platform to speak the truth.
Saying YES could strip shame from your life.
Saying YES could cost you everything.
Saying YES will be worth it.
Saying YES will restore you to the heart of the Father.
Saying YES moves you bravely forward. Every single time.

At the heart of it all, the YES Life is about letting go of ourselves.

As I have dug deep to finish a book, I'm not sure I even like it or would read it. That's honest. And so because I don't feel it, I have had to put myself aside to get on with the job, say YES to something I know I just need to do, and finish, regardless of how I feel about it or whether it's good enough.

19 | WHAT IS THE YES LIFE?

James Clear says:

'It doesn't matter how good or how bad it is. You don't need to set the world on fire with your first try. You just need to prove to yourself that you have what it takes to produce something. There are no artists, athletes, entrepreneurs or scientists who became great by half-finishing their work. Stop debating what you should make and just make something.'

I wonder how many times I have sat at the junction of YES and missed the thrill of the ride ahead because I didn't quite see the perfect outline or outcome. I'm sure there are many, too many.

The YES Life is about pioneering. Pioneering is the *'laid-down life,'* as Nate Johnstone said. At the core of the YES Life is this beckoning to pioneer something new and bring a fresh focus and a new vision to life. Pioneers carry a divine blueprint and respond with YES to what they instinctively know is God calling them forward.

Pioneers blaze trails and live their lives 'at all costs'. They say YES when it makes no sense, when the timing is off, when the bank accounts are empty, and when the politics is most uncertain. Pioneers run ahead because they see that the YES Life is not just for them but also for the world around them. Pioneers refuse to live in fear. They do it afraid and move bravely forward. As Dylan has taught me, pioneers know what it means to live like Isaac and sow even in famine.

We had a dream of a church building. Not just any building. A campus dream. Think Google, but better. A place where people could find a home to belong every day of the week, even beyond a Sunday. A place that could house the pillars of society and where the church is at the epicentre. Where all kinds of people would find themselves interacting and doing life together. I loved to listen to his dreams, but I could not picture a campus. At that time, we were meeting in a fruit-packing shed. It smelled. It was often damp from the rain, and we got scorched in the heat. We had to contend with insufficient parking, monkeys, mongooses, and much mud. When he showed me his sketches and sold me stories of the dream, I tended to listen from a place of kind interest rather than pioneering faith.

In 2012, the realities of all this planning and dreaming, his YES and drive to see the vision God gave him, came to be. We purchased land and started talking about a building project. There was just one problem. He'd assured me we wouldn't build a church building and have a baby simultaneously. That didn't happen. Honor was well on her way, and the more I grew in size, the faster the bricks rose from the ground.

Pioneers say YES at great cost to themselves and others. The YES Life may trample on our perfect picture of how it should all work out, but at the crux of it all is this inclination to say YES anyway.

The day I went into labour, Dylan got a call to say that our building project had been suspended due to a glitch in our plans. It may have seemed like a disaster to many, but for me, I got to have my third baby without a building going up, just like Dylan had promised. The construction resumed in January after she was born, just four months later. Some say that it was a win-win.

The YES Life does not have a definite structure and rock-solid plan. Pioneering comes with challenges, but I would rather have the YES

Life than a safe life where I never took a swing at the things that keep my heart ablaze.

I spent far too many years playing it safe, never trying anything new or brave because I was worried about what it looked like.

Will people like it?
Will people read it?
Will people reject me?
Will this ruin my reputation?
Will this cost me relationships?

At the end of the day, none of this is relevant.

What matters is that we will look back at our lives and know confidently that we gave it everything we had. We said YES to the YES Life. I said YES. I established something. I became someone. I went after the visions and dreams in my heart. I stayed married, and beyond that, I fought for a beautiful marriage. I believed in my husband and breathed life and courage into his soul. I raised four children despite the world telling me I was ruining the environment. I pioneered a new day for my children that will affect generations and generations to come; I believed in the church when people said I could do other things better and make more money elsewhere. I fought for a movement of women that championed each other outside of feminist ideology. I remained grateful when the odds were stacked against me. I showed up when I was spent. I was bold even when I wasn't entirely sure. I pioneered. I blazed a new path.

I want to be able to say these things.

I want to look back and know I said YES to the YES Life – the YES Life that God invited me to live.

The YES Life is an assignment that all of us are presented with. One that will give us more authority, territory, and inheritance beyond what we can ask or think of.

Do you dare to let everything go for the sake of living the YES Life?

20 | The Key Principles of the YES Life

Principles are ideas or beliefs that guide us. Certain principles help move us bravely forward in the YES Life.

YES is a spirit.
YES starts in your gut.
YES helps to sharpen your instincts.
YES is something you choose. Over and over again.
YES is a power word.
YES is shaped by your words.
YES is something you carry everywhere you go.
YES enables you to be led by peace.
YES sets you free.
YES is living with the belief that the best is yet to come.
YES is hard.
YES is holy.
YES is right.
YES is good.
YES enables you to lean towards YES every time.
YES releases you to say no to something so you can say YES to something else.
YES is about letting go.
YES will cause you to let go of seeking perfection.
YES will help you to let go of control.
YES releases you from bitterness.

YES kills the thief of comparison.
YES frees you from shame.
YES frees you from fear.
YES moves you beyond your circumstances.
YES ushers in mercy.
YES enables your wholeness.
YES brings healing.
YES redeems.
YES unlocks love.
YES causes change.
YES ensures a fulfilled life.
YES opens you up to grace.
YES ensures you learn.
YES will make you laugh.
YES will make you do it afraid.
YES will ensure you grow.
YES is a thoughtful response.
YES is a conduit.
YES is more.
YES is infinite.
YES is unlimited.
YES is opportunistic.
YES is big and bold.
YES is risky.
YES thrives without hesitation.
YES is powerful.
YES is the catalyst for more YESES to be said.
YES is contagious.
YES has a ripple effect.

20 | THE KEY PRINCIPLES OF THE YES LIFE

YES cannot be lost.

YES cannot be taken from us.

YES pursues us.

YES is for life.

At the heart of this YES Life is this simple truth:

You've got to know yourself to be yourself.

You've got to be yourself to give yourself away.

YES is giving yourself away.

21 | An everyday YES Life

If you are anything like me, you are fundamentally human to your core, and within that humanness is the child within you – the dreamer, the idealist. You believe that life can be magical and full of adventure, and perhaps, like me, you've even lived your life with crazy, innocent faith that thinks you can have it all.

If you're anything like me, life got hard along the way. Harder than you expected it to be. At times, it's been dark and lonely. You've tasted what it is to be force-fed grief. You have failed. And yet, like me, you have refused to accept that this is where it ends. You believe that the story is simply not over. That there is always more. That YES moments are lying in your future.

If you're anything like me, you may have found alternative ways to cope. You have signed peace treaties with demons from your past. In desperation, you've had to reach out for a lifeline that saves you. Like me, you've felt everything, from disappointment to shame. You've walked through the seasons of fog, hoping to attain a clear vision and wondered where you will turn next. However, in and through it all, you have held onto God-sized expectations like me. Not in something, but in Someone – someone far more powerful than you could ever imagine – the One who places the YES Life invitations into our lives.

If you're anything like me, you have learned the gravity and brevity of this life – that it can take your breath away. Yet, you are still crazy enough to believe that God Himself flings open great, big doors of opportunity – moments, people, and stories that call for your YES.

'He will open doors no man can shut and shut doors no man can open.' – Revelation 3:7

Living the YES Life calls for us to live in tension. It calls for a brave move forward.

On the one hand, we live with a somewhat naive outlook, believing that something extraordinary can happen at any stage. We can say YES to Someone and something far bigger than we ever thought possible. On the other hand, we're faced with real life that threatens us almost daily. I said YES to something great, and… here I remain. *Surely this can't be it? Will I always feel like this? Is this how far I'll go? Will I forever be friends with the familiarity of my failures and shortcomings? Is there not more?*

The YES Life is not a problem to be solved but rather something to be managed daily.
It may look like an opportunity and a grand adventure, but most everyday life does not. The YES Life is solidified in a moment, but then a steady walk follows, one foot in front of the other – every day.

The liturgical calendar has a window of time called 'ordinary time.' This period lives outside of and between Easter and Christmas. It's not

21 | AN EVERYDAY YES LIFE

that it has no significance; it's just everyday life. It sits in the middle of time and, at its core, is an 'ordinary-ness' that can often be overlooked.

Ordinary time is a time of growth. The seed is sitting in the warmth of the ground. It's a slow and sometimes painful time. A time for maturing. It's where the mystery unfolds, and we're found in the waiting places. It's seemingly monotonous. In this space, we learn what our unfolding YES looks like.

In his Praying the Bible, Philip Reinders says it well:
'Ordinary doesn't mean boring or second rate but simply every day.' [40]

There will always be the grand YES moments. There are many throughout our lives, but the ordinary time is when we take hold of the implications of our YES. We allow our YES to take shape and form in our coming, going, waking, and sleeping. This is when our YES makes a critical connection with our everyday lives.

Life is an ongoing process that starts and ends with this undefined, varying length of time positioned in the middle. It's undeniably dull at times. We don't shoot the lights out living in the glorious YES once said; instead, we commit to outworking the reality of it daily.

I said YES to marriage. I now live within the 'ordinary time' of that YES: decisions to put someone else first, commitments to see another always, the choice to reach my hand across the bed signalling an invitation to move closer, listening and learning, prioritisation and communication, the ebb and flow of want and need.

I said YES to children. I now function consistently within the 'ordinary time' of four times YESES said: carpools, shows, sports games, school lunches, hugs upon hugs, doctors' visits, worn knees from daily prayers, moment-by-moment reminders to hold fast to the values of our home, weekly check-ins, nighttime stories, manners, training, conversations, hard ones, sorry, and forgiveness.

I said YES to the church. I now pour out daily within the 'ordinary time' of that YES: Prayer moments. Hours spent building lessons that will form children's spirituality. Study and worship. Hard and holy conversations. Late nights. Weddings and funerals. Tears and great joy. Questions and calling. Community and disappointment. A whole lot of staying and even more releasing.

I said YES to lead. I now live in the 'ordinary time' that looks like daily work and choosing the higher ground. To journey the road less travelled and navigate the well-worn ancient paths of faith. Leadership indeed does *'suck'*, as John Maxwell so eloquently articulated. The higher you get, the less options you have. Conflict management. Little margin. Big decisions. Humble thoughtfulness even when I just want to be right.

I said YES to women. I now line up with the 'ordinary time' of pursuing their value every day. I seek out women in every stage of life. I make space for the widows and encourage new mothers. I welcome home the teenagers. Moments upon moments, I fight comparison and pull others towards the same end. Despite what I see, I challenge the ways of old and believe that the world will look considerably more unified for my daughters in the future.

I said YES to pain – to a nothing missing, nothing lacking kind of life. I now live in the 'ordinary time' where choosing to face the pain of the past and present is embraced and nurtured because I refuse to allow it to show up in an unhealthy way further down the line. I acknowledge it, and I look it in the eyes. It is not who I am but what I am going through. I respond with kindness to myself so that I can do that for others, too.

It is impossible to consistently choose someone or something if you don't fully believe it is worth it. Nothing worthwhile is easy. When we sit in the middle of the night where doubt and fear set in, this is where conviction matters. Is our YES worth it all? When we can't see the way through, and the darkness threatens the YES Life, will we be able to keep standing?

Every YES requires our commitment and dedication. Every YES needs to be absorbed and assimilated into the story of our lives. With every YES said comes the reality of establishing the YES within our ordinary time because if it is not established, there is every possibility we'll give it up. We must choose YES and go all in despite the risk that it may not work out. Establishing your YES looks like saying it, regardless of what it looks like. YES, you may fail, but not without a fight. An established YES allows you to do it afraid and step forward despite your heart's uncertainty.

YES has demanded more from me than I ever thought I could give. It has built a resilient spirit in me where I refuse to give up because of a hard day. I will not allow fear to have the final say. I will not bow down to my insecurity. I will not let the uncertainty of what I do not know hold me back.

Your YES will call more from you than you ever imagined. It will stretch you. It will unravel you. It will strengthen you to the core and demand you come along for the adventure. If your YES is worth it, it is worth everything. Every single part of you. Every molecule and atom.

Your YES may ask you to lose everything to gain everything. Jump in. Fling your arms wide open and SAY YES.

Now that you're this far into this book let's talk about how you can establish your YES.

Five steps to say YES to the YES Life:

Step 1: Keep saying YES.

Step 2: Refer to step 1.

Step 3. Refer to step 2.

Step 4: Refer to step 3.

Step 5: Refer to step 4.

You get it now, right?

22 | No is a Full Sentence

I've always fought against paradoxes. I don't like them. Statements like *'You must spend money to make money'* or *'This is the beginning of the end'* have always annoyed me. They highlight a tension I need to manage, and as you may have gathered from chapters before, I struggle to live in tension.

The tension between YES and no was so difficult for me to understand that I tried to sabotage myself and the life I believe God has invited me into. I simply could not reconcile that my commitment to YES would demand that I learn to say no.

I wrestled with this question: *How could I find the courage to distinguish between 'no' and 'YES' when I felt called to lean towards YES?*

I thought that the YES Life made no room for no, but I discovered over time that sometimes you have to say no to one thing so that you can say YES to another. A no is not necessarily the endpoint. A no is not always a period. A no is not an inhibitor. No has the potential to be a gateway.

Sometimes, our best YES will demand a wise and strategic no.

There have been many moments where I have had to take stock of where I am and who I am surrounded by. I've had to look closely at my habits, address my thoughts, and assess how I spend my time. I've looked and observed while considering the implications.

Will I walk into the YES Life if I continue here?
Is this for me?
Why am I doing this?
What lies beneath this behaviour?

I have said no to friendships.
I have said no to voices.
I have said no to environments.
I have said no to songs.
I have said no to habits.
I have said no to conversations.
I have said no to invitations.
I have said no to opportunities.

I have said no, again and again, so I could take hold of the YES Life waiting before me.
'Choose today', says God. (Deuteronomy 30:19) It's taken me a while to figure this out. When invited to live the YES Life, we are always given the freedom and privilege to choose. Sometimes, choosing the YES Life means saying no.

In 2019, Dylan presented a vision for our year: *'Leaving much for more.'* It was incredible to see how many of us said no to things that year so we could say YES to others. It seemed that we could sense the beckoning of 'more' found within saying YES to God, and to take hold of more, we would need to leave some things behind.

A no can be challenging to understand and costly. However, it is also an obedient word, and obedience is uncomfortable.

As a young twenty-something newly saved and excitable Christian, I soon realised that old habits die hard. Some things were easy to say goodbye to; others were not. For some reason, I couldn't let go of late nights, drinks in dark spaces, and far too many unhelpful conversations. I struggled to move away from this party lifestyle until I saw the stark reality that my friends, who had not made the same decision as I had, were having on my decision. They didn't understand my newfound fascination with church. They didn't understand my need to hang out with those 'strange church people.' I learnt a defining lesson the hard way early on in my adulthood: *'We become the company that we keep.'*

I couldn't resist my unhealthy habits because everyone around me encouraged them. I wasn't making life-giving choices because I wasn't secure and strong enough to say no to the crowd. I had to say no to my friends and say YES to pursuing a life of faith.

No is the gateway to a better YES. It creates room and margin for the YES we long to say. The right no brings forth the best YES.

My greatest struggle was learning how to say no. I always felt like I needed to explain myself and justify my choices. I grew tremendously when I stumbled along the profound words of author and psychologist Henry Cloud, who says in his book Boundaries, *'No is a full sentence.'*[41]

No is enough. A confident 'no' further aligns us with the YES we are committed to saying. Sometimes, there will be a need for elaboration and communication around why we are saying no. In these moments, Steven Furtick says, *'Choose to be known for what you are for rather than what you're against.'* Basically, he's saying talk about your YES over the no.

When my no is challenged, I present **my** convictions. I bring my YES to the table. Our lean towards YES makes all the difference, even when saying no.

YES is my resolution. Because I believe in YES, I am willing to say no. Saying no takes great courage, but it enables an even greater YES.

Accept that you may not be included.
Accept that you may miss opportunities.
Accept that criticism may find its way to you.
Accept the feeling of being misunderstood.
Accept negative feedback.

Make peace with your YES and discover the no that needs to be said along the way. Move bravely forward.

23 | The YES Effect

When one person says YES, it also catalyses others to say theirs.

In an article released by Forbes in 2021, Pankaj Srivastava released his thoughts on the power of YES in teams.

He outlined how the experience of saying YES causes us to become better thinkers. When an opportunity or idea is presented, we are forced to think about the implications of saying YES or no. He gives examples and makes a case for how team members would hear YES, pushing them to go further and higher in their tasks and abilities. In his opinion, saying YES breeds more solutions and higher standards. YES allows conversions and strategising to continue, while no stops everything in its tracks. One person's YES pulls everyone else to consider theirs, which makes all the difference.

Srivastava wrote: *'If you look deeper, you might realise that many successful people have been open to new thinking and risk-taking others would not. The irony is that successful people, who are often highly focused on their vision, are also mindful of the fact that there is much greater risk when you don't veer off from the chosen path and don't take risks from time to time. They have realised that to achieve awesome results; they must say YES to empower new ideas, push boundaries and discover possibilities.*

I have used the 'YES mindset' for over 12 years, which has served me well. Here are my tips for adopting the mindset: First, move away from being a decision-maker and orient yourself to learn. Ask, "What can I learn from this conversation?" Second, don't raise objections – instead, ask more questions such as, "What will I need to do to make this successful?" I've learned there is power in saying YES, even to unconventional ideas. Realising this was a breakthrough for me. In my experience, most people falsely believe that saying no is the quicker, more efficient method for staying focused and moving faster. While it is crucial to determine where to focus our time and resources, often making it prudent to say no, it is essential first to stay in the YES mindset. Without a YES mindset, your first reaction is to disregard new thoughts. You train yourself to be risk-averse. Good ideas can come from anyone or anywhere; be open to receiving them. [42]

The more I read about this man's thoughts about the power of YES in teams, the more fascinated I became. Perhaps saying YES is somewhat contagious? Could my choosing this YES Life have caused others to do the same?

I was once sent a video entitled *Leadership Lessons from a Dancing Guy*. It's ridiculous and profound all at the same time. A *lone man begins to dance on a hill of people and makes a few simple moves to a catchy beat that no one is paying attention to. He's just doing what he feels like, and then his YES to the onlooker becomes intriguing. Something interesting happens next. In comes the first follower. The guy who holds a YES inside himself but is slightly less confident to step out alone. The video then takes a turn. People from all over the hillside join the dance. The crowd begins to grow, and suddenly, everyone moves and shakes with the freedom most of us dream of.*

23 | THE YES EFFECT

This short clip sums up the reality of what I like to call the YES effect. It takes one YES and an unlikely first responder to say YES, and the entire community is suddenly on board.

A radical, courageous, and obedient YES will inspire action in others. This is the nature of pioneering. When we step out, others will also follow and say their YES.

Over the past few years, many people have affirmed my decision to say YES. They've done so by telling me stories of how my YES catalysed theirs. This fascinated me as I could not understand why my YES held such weight. I then realised that it was not about my YES but rather about the power of YES in and of itself.

YES holds the power.
YES stimulates thinking.
YES instils courage.
YES fuels the fire.
YES does the work.
YES inspires.
YES challenges.
YES calls forth.
YES creates and sustains a ripple effect.
YES calls forth another YES.

Some of my friends, fellow church workers and authors shared how my YES gave them the courage to say theirs. This is the joy of YES in friendship. This is the strength of YES within a community. This is the YES effect.

NANDE'S STORY

'Is maturing possible in isolation? Does it take authentic conversation and involved friendship to give maturity a chance? Is there a mutual benefit in saying YES to friendship? Wisdom literature in the Bible speaks of iron sharpening iron in Proverbs 27:17. It suggests we can sharpen one another's gifts or stir each other to exercise them.

I met Tes Jahnig in 2019 when she launched the Awakening Sisterhood Conference. She had sent a beautiful invitation for me to come and speak at the conference. That invitation persuaded me it had to have been God because I couldn't think of any possible reason for her to invite me at that time, with my knowledge and experience in sharing the Gospel. I remember feeling nervous because I had never been to Ballito. I've often considered that initial visit to Linc Church as my first time meeting the Jahnigs while forgetting it was their first time meeting me. Not only that, but I know that Tes is responsible in every area of her existence. She stewards the Sisterhood community with grand passion and sensitivity to the Holy Spirit. I now understand that her YES on that occasion had considerable implications for my life. Her response to God triggered my reply. An interesting thing happens once we respond to living out who God has made us to be. We become aware of what we don't know yet. We grow into an awareness of our areas that call for a bit of sharpening or maturing. We realise more and more our imperfections and limitations. Depending on your interpretation of your oneness with Christ and the message of grace, this can cause you to hide or catapult you to an adventurous course of learning. Tes' YES keeps me saying YES. My sojourn of accepting grace began at the meeting with my dear friend, Tes.

Since I met the Jahnig family, I've been curious about their generosity and lifestyle of gratitude. I've discovered that such deep gratitude is only fueled, shaped, and sustained by the Gospel of Jesus Christ. Tes has understood the Gospel. It's no surprise that her YES would be catalytic, overflowing into her marriage, parenting, ministry and friendships – even into the life of a girl, Nande Boss, from a small town called Cradock.

Tes' YES Life has offered me insight into the way forward as God's daughter. I'll never take for granted her generosity in sharing her platforms and friendships with me. Tes' YES contributed to me living boldly and freely in my calling. To move towards a full revelation of grace.'

KELLY'S STORY

'The courageous and daily act of saying YES to a vision to build a local church with a substantial value for family and community has radically transformed our lives individually and as a family. The seeds that the Linc story has sowed into our children's lives are massively producing fruit in their teenage years! Their deep convictions to live a God-centred life as young people in this generation are wholeheartedly attributed to the years of growing up in the context of the Linc story. Linc did something radical in its time when it made church a fun, attractive, and inspiring place, and what was seen and felt was unique and left an imprint on our souls. We are confident that because they know what a healthy church, family and community look like, they will not settle for second best as they strive to live lives of purity and freedom in their generation.

Being close friends with Tes has been one of our greatest gifts. We have watched every small and big YES create a legacy that the whole community lives in the wake of. Husbands and wives, sons and daughters, have all seen a bigger God story in their own lives because of Linc's constant inspired call to gather, be equipped and then mobilised in the world.

I AM, my Leadership Development Company, has been birthed because of this call. Tes' YES gave me the courage to believe that I had a ministry to activate, and I am privileged to partner with God and be the custodian of His work in the world. I give credit to being a part of a community that calls one to go deeper and further than one can believe possible. As Tes has continued in the God call over her life and has continued to say YES, she has unlocked courage in all of us to believe that there is a greater God story *that awaits us all. She has allowed us to dare to believe that there is more and to keep moving forward no matter what to attain it.*

Our family feels incredible honour and gratitude for all that has been sacrificed and pioneered in the Linc Church story because we live in the fruit of it!

God has always highlighted this scripture in my heart for Tes: "Be sure to welcome our friend Phoebe in the way of the Master, with all the generous hospitality we Christians are famous for. I heartily endorse both her and her work. She's a vital representative of the church at Cenchrea. Help her out in whatever she asks. She deserves anything you can do for her. She's helped many people, including me!" Romans 16:1-2'

GILLIAN'S STORY

'Never doubt the effectiveness of a church, a body designed by God to look like Jesus to encourage, build, comfort, and equip each other.

Tes' heart to trust God and believe in His goodness and faithfulness enables her to lead with an open-handed posture that positioned me in a time in my life when I knew there was more but didn't fully believe in myself and was way too concerned about people's opinions and how things should look.

Her natural, organic and Holy Spirit-led life opened my heart to a powerful YES to believe that what I had to say carried value and weight in the coaching/ counselling world that is my passion.

Never did she prescribe or even name what she was doing, yet the spirit she carries naturally unfolded and imparted how God sees me. She has called me and encouraged me to step out into the God dream I wanted but never thought I could have.

Her desire to say YES uncomplicatedly with what she held in her heart and hands catalysed and launched me towards my YES.

I am grateful to God for His body, His gift to the church in the person of Tes and our Father in Heaven who caused our paths to cross.'

23 | THE YES EFFECT

JACI'S STORY

'They say, "Courage is not the absence of fear, but pressing on despite it." Since I've known Tes, she has embodied courage. When she is broken, when she is empty, when she is full of life and roaring into battle, Tes says, 'YES!' to what God is calling her into. I love that.

The first 'YES' of Tes that affected my life was her 'YES' to celebrating others. She took comparison by the balls (can I say that?) and decided to celebrate every woman who made her feel inferior in any way. In doing so, she grew, and so did her world. I have endeavoured to follow her in this courageous habit.

The second 'YES' of Tes was her 'YES' to fighting for other women. I attended her first Sisterhood and asked her if I could use the name (to which she said… 'YES!'). I then launched a Sisterhood of our own. Her zeal for setting women free and into space and inviting them to sit at the table inspired me and set me on a path in ministry to women.

The third 'YES' of Tes that comes to mind is probably the one that changed my life the most. Tes loves the Church. She loves the global Church and the local church. She refused to sit by and allow her leadership gift to atrophy because she was a woman or because her kids were still filling her arms and her days. Tes said 'YES' to leadership in the church when a lot of us girls were still not sure if that was a thing. She took her seat at the table, found her voice, grew in skill, and, for her faithfulness, she was rewarded with an increase in gift and anointing. It was beautiful, and I knew I had to find the courage to do the same. Her example and encouragement helped me to do so.'

THE YES LIFE

What would it look like for you to move bravely forward today?

To acknowledge your YES?

To say it boldly and with confidence?

What if the YES you long to say could stir up courage in someone else to say theirs?

What if your YES Life was the seed of the YES effect in your world?

24 | It's Still YES

It was an ordinary Monday morning. Dylan was away preaching at our dear friend's church, and I was up early to ensure everyone was ready for a new week. Being a mindful millennial, I try to ignore my phone in the morning. It's set to Do Not Disturb mode, yet miraculously, my mother bypassed this function at six o'clock that morning.

She did not often call me at this stage of our lives, leaving me to navigate my life and family as she enjoyed the 'latter years' with my Dad.

Why call me at six o'clock?

Instinctively, as I looked at my phone, I knew. My Dad.

As I answered the phone, I heard the words:

Your Dad. It's not good. Pray, Tessie, pray.

Surrounded by my children, I fell on my knees and begged God for another minute. Please, Jesus, don't do THIS. My mind has since blanked out most of this moment. I was told that my children had called our neighbour, a long-time friend, and she had arrived so I could get to my parents' home.

I arrived as the paramedics were urgently and consistently working hard to try and save his life. I was late to the scene; tragically, it was too late for our family.

My Dad had woken struggling for breath and suffered a fatal heart attack that almost instantly took his life. Only a miracle could have saved him. I will never understand why we didn't get this miracle that day. And I have resolved that I will live with this unanswered question here on earth.

I said goodbye to my Dad that day. I sat with him as his body cooled and told him how magnificent he was.

I told him that he should rest knowing we will live strong and continue, not because we can but because we have to and we have a future hope to hang on to.

I told him we would care for my mom and that life would be full of him. We'd continue to celebrate. Every birthday. Every milestone. Every year. We'd continue to live alive because that was how he lived, and that would bring him honour.

I will forever be proud of him. He is my hero, and the standard of fathering he set was wonderfully high.

It was about three hours of sitting and waiting before his body was taken from us. And in that moment, watching that car drive away, part of me died too. Because you see, death is not for us. We weren't created with death in mind. Everything the Father intended was life and life in abundance. *Life is real. Life is earnest. And the grave is not the goal.*

Dust thou art dust, to dust returnest, was not spoken of the soul. – Henry Wadsworth Longfellow[43]

As I watched the bedrock of my earthly existence be physically removed from my life, I felt like I was at the end – the end of an era, the end of myself.

Why is this significant? Why do I share this brutally difficult memory?

There will come a time when we all will have our YES and the life that follows it dismantled right before our eyes. We'll question what we're doing and why we are here. We'll start rethinking the fabric of what we are made of. It will feel like the scaffolding we've stood upon for years needs to come down, and the process of unravelling will leave us undone. It may happen because of tragedy or trauma. It may happen because we've abdicated from the YES Life invitation. It may come from choices we shouldn't have made or relationships that cost us the YES we wished we could move bravely towards.

I'm not sure what shook you to your core; perhaps that day is still coming. For me, it was this moment when my Dad left this earth and embarked on the journey home to the place where a room had been prepared for him.

This loss is significant because my relationship with my father was special. Our connection was unique. We had an affection for one another, and I lived in the glow of his pride and joy. I knew I was the apple of his eye. His lap was always open for me, and I could instinctively comprehend what safety meant because he allowed me to rest my head on his heart.

In an instant, life now existed without him. Who would hug me for a bit longer every time? Who would I call when I needed something fixed? Who would teach my son about farming, machinery and fishing? Who would argue with me about politics and the media? Who would pocket-dial me daily? Who would drape their arm over my shoulder and pull me close for no other reason than just because? Who would beam when I preached? Who would tell me my kids are good kids? Whose eyes would twinkle when they laughed?

In the early days following his death, I would sit in the corner of our couch with tea and a blanket in the darkness and quiet of the morning. I felt completely and utterly alone. Abandoned by God.

There were only three questions I had in those defining moments:
What now, God?
Who will I be in this moment?
Who do I want to become from this?

As I look back, I see now that it was in this space of raw, unfiltered grief that I drew a line in the sand. I didn't know what I was doing; I just did what was instinctive. I cried out to God. I needed Him like I had never needed Him before. He met me and called me bravely forward. And in that desperate space, I made a choice.

I would not get stuck.
I would say YES to pursuing union with God passionately.
I would say YES to being in community.
I would not hide in my mourning.
My answer was still YES. YES to The YES Life.

24 | IT'S STILL YES

Looking back, I had no idea what the implications of these quiet couch moments were. I now see they were defining moments as the reality of grieving set in, and I began the hard and holy work of mourning someone I loved.

Mourning and grief are unlike any other process we go through. We don't want it, we don't choose it, yet it forces its way inside our hearts and homes like an unwelcome guest. It takes up residence and forces us to face what we do not want to face: our loss.

Initially, I fought it in my heart and wrestled it in my soul. But, thankfully, my body and soul would not release me from the job at hand. I had no control over my tears, my sorrow or my rage. I functioned automatically and methodically, and even my attempts to 'stay busy' were no match for grief.

Everywhere I went, it found me, early in the morning or late at night. It arrived on a Monday every week and showed up loud and intrusive on the 28th of every month. I so wished someone could take it from me and do the work on my behalf. Through those arduous days, I learnt that grieving my Dad was something I could only do for myself. It was not something I could or should delegate; it would invite me to honour and love my Dad in his absence. It was an unwelcome gift but a gift for me to receive nonetheless.

As time passed, I became more acquainted with and settled in my grief. I made peace with it and welcomed the process with open arms. Somehow, I knew this was one of the most holy things I would ever do – a process that would tune my ear to the voice of Heaven and fix my gaze on Jesus and only Jesus.

I find myself, even two years later, unwilling to hand my grief over for the convenience and comfort of others. I will cry when I cry. I will speak when I speak. I will bring the nature of this loss daily to my Jesus and ask Him to cover me with his cloak as I navigate the way through.

Throughout that time, one of the most frustrating and difficult realities was that I struggled to complete this book. Writing hurt. My fingers were frozen, and my heart ached. It was just too painful and calling from me more than I knew I had to give.

On another trip to Israel just over a year after the loss of my Dad, I heard the whisper of the Holy Spirit once more to pick up this piece of work again.

'Write the book, Tes; use your words; let them fall like seeds to the ground.'

This was the daily echo that resounded in me as I walked the dusty desert roads and toured the ancient paths that felt the footsteps of my Saviour.

I needed to say YES even in my grief. I returned to South Africa, got off the plane, and called an editor I knew would hold me to account and get me over the finish line of a developmental edit. Knowing it or not, she would partner with God in leading me forward in obedience and faith.

At a similar time, I spent regular afternoons at my mom's home when I noticed her many orchids waiting to bloom again. Most of them she had been gifted over my Dad's death, and the flowerless plants resonated with what I felt was the state of my soul.

I'd seen a hanging orchid garden at a friend's guest house and instantly thought: I want one. I asked my mom for two sad-looking stems, and when I got home, I strapped them to a tree and left them with no flowers or beauty. Barren. Wasted. They looked like I felt, and I found some satisfaction in that. They represented my book dream, which felt impossible by the day.

It was while I was wrestling the final pages at my dining room table that I spotted it out of the corner of my eye. The blossom of something new. Yellow and bright. A signpost. A signal. A declaration that winter was over. Colour was here. Life was here.

Maybe I was crazy, or perhaps I just needed a sign. Who knows? But this blooming orchid told me that my YES Life is still here. He is making all things new. Nothing is wasted. Roads and rivers bursting forth. Spring is dawning. My soul leapt with joy as I saw it.

Forget about what's happened;
don't keep going over old history.
Be alert, be present. I'm about to do something brand-new.
It's bursting out! Don't you see it?
There it is! I'm making a road through the desert,
rivers in the wastelands. – Isaiah 43:18-19 MSG

I have grappled with the notion of moving bravely forward from this defining moment in my life. It feels wrong, like I am forgetting my Dad.

Logically, I know this is not the case, but I have had to keep reminding myself that I will never forget my Dad or what happened. How could I? To forget would be dishonouring and discredit his profound role in my life. No, I can not forget. I choose YES. I choose YES to remember him. I choose YES to feel the pain of losing and grieving him. I choose YES to acknowledge all that can be learned from loss.

At the heart of this story is the golden thread of His big YES seen in every season of my life, enabling and encouraging my YES in return.

So, despite every desert and every valley, despite myself, even now, even as I question where all of this should end, I know, like I know, like I know – I may not know what is around the corner, I will not have all the answers, and yet, even then, I still choose YES.

YES to God.
YES to marriage.
YES to children.
YES to lead.
YES to the Church.
YES to gratitude.
YES to doing it, afraid.
YES to embracing it all.

It is always YES.

Conclusion: This is Just the Beginning

Honestly, I don't know how to end this book. I think it is supposed to feel somewhat unfinished because this means I get to continue the story and grow into The YES Life more and more – year on year.

As you close this book, I want you to know YES is possible for your life.

You have what it takes to say YES to the YES Life.

Don't let anyone tell you otherwise.

Don't tell yourself the story of no.

And when it gets hard, when you are unsure, when you can't see the YES in front of you, would you hear the sound of my voice saying:

I value you. I see you. I believe in you.

I know that your YES is necessary for all of us to live in the fullness of the YES Life.

May my words empower you to believe that you can and will say YES.

Say it. YES. Then, keep saying it again.

YES to moving bravely forward.

YES… to The YES Life.

Thank You

Dear friends

I made it. There were days, even to this point, when I thought I never would. Editing exposes, and it is brutal to endure. I have questioned myself and my ability so many times I exhausted myself and probably those closest to me.

I want to thank those of you who pushed me to the end. In particular, I want to mention Amber. Without her encouragement, kindness, strategy, and brilliant mind, this book categorically would not have been published and printed. Thank you, Ambs, for saying YES to God and, in turn, YES to me. I will forever be grateful for the way you so effortlessly pushed me towards obedience to what God has asked me to do.
I hope to cheer you on in similar endeavours in the future.

To every reader, thank you for your generosity of spirit. I am humbled that anyone would read my work, let alone purchase it and share it with their world.

I would love to hear how this book has impacted your life, so please remember to send me all the emails, DMs, messages, and voice notes. I value your feedback and stories.

Until the next one… Keep saying YES.

All my love, Tes

Endnotes

1. Dillard, A. (2013). *The Writing Life*. Harper Perennial.
2. Clare, C. (2015). *City of Glass*. Margaret K. McElderry Books.
3. Frankl, V. E. (1997). *Man's Search for Meaning*. Simon & Schuster.
4. Genesis 22:1
5. Ortberg, J. (2015). *All the Places to Go… How Will You Know? God Has Placed Before You an Open Door. What Will You Do?* Tyndale House.
6. Queen Elizabeth I's speech to the troops at Tilbury (1588).
7. Psalm 30:5
8. Revelation 1:18
9. Spafford, H. (1876). *It is Well With My Soul*.
10. Hillsong UNITED. (2013). Oceans (Where Feet May Fail).
11. 2 Samuel 7:16 NIV
12. Gates, M. (2019). *The moment of lift: How empowering women changes the world*. Flatiron Books.
13. Gates, M. (2019). *The moment of lift: How empowering women changes the world*. Flatiron Books.
14. James 1:1-4 TPT
15. James 1:2 NIV
16. Lusko, L. (2015). *Through the eyes of a lion: Facing impossible pain, finding incredible power*. Thomas Nelson.
17. Galatians 6:2 NIV
18. Voskamp, A. (2012). *One thousand gifts devotional: Reflections on finding everyday graces*. Zondervan.
19. Voskamp, A. (2012). *One thousand gifts devotional: Reflections on finding everyday graces*. Zondervan.
20. Philippians 4:8 NIV
21. Proverbs 23:7 NIV
22. Leaf, C. (2015). *Switch on your brain: The key to peak happiness, thinking, and health*. Baker Academic.
23. Voskamp, A. (2012). *One thousand gifts devotional: Reflections on finding everyday graces*. Zondervan.

24 Rolheiser, R. (2014). *Holy longing, the* (15th ed.). Bantam Doubleday Dell Publishing Group.
25 *John 14:12 NIV*
26 Matthew 7:14
27 Acts 16:6-10
28 Stanley, A. (2005). *Visioneering: God's blueprint for developing and maintaining vision.* Multnomah Press.
29 Proverbs 29:18 KJV
30 Brown, B. (2015). *Daring greatly: How the courage to be vulnerable transforms the way we live, love, parent, and lead.* Penguin Life.
31 Lee, H. (1960). *To Kill a Mockingbird.* Grand Central Publishing.
32 Esther 4:14
33 Furtick, S. (2021, September 8). *Faith doesn't take the weight off your life, it shows you how to handle it.* [Facebook post]. Facebook. https://www.facebook.com/StevenFurtick/posts/faith-doesnt-take-the-weight-off-your-life-it-shows-you-how-to-handle-it/4529903243697722/
34 1 Samuel 30:6
35 Colossians 1:27
36 Proverbs 18:21
37 Luke 6:45; Matthew 12:34
38 2 Corinthians 10:5
39 Matthew 7:14
40 Reinders, P. F. (2012). *Seeking god's face: Praying with the bible through the year.* Faith Alive Christian Resources.
41 Cloud, H., & Townsend, J. (2017). *Boundaries updated and expanded edition: When to say yes, how to say no to take control of your life.* Zondervan.
42 Srivastava, P. (2021, May 17). *The power of yes: Why the yes mindset leads to innovation and creates great leaders.* Forbes. https://www.forbes.com/sites/forbesbusinesscouncil/2021/05/17/the-power-of-yes-why-the-yes-mindset-leads-to-innovation-and-creates-great-leaders/
43 Longfellow, H. W. (2017). A *Psalm of life (classic reprint).* Forgotten Books.

Connect with Tes

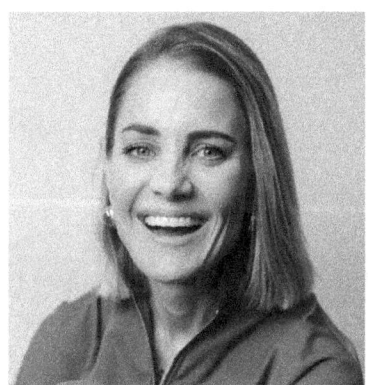

Tes Jahnig is a daughter, sister, wife and mother who, alongside her husband Dylan, leads Linc Church and the Linc Sisterhood. Tes lives to say YES to God and endeavours to use every opportunity of influence to live and serve people of every generation with the Word of God.

She believes that healthy families and thriving churches that have Jesus at their centre hold the power to change the world. Every day is another gift for Tes, and when she's not surrounded by women, you'll find her with children – her four beautiful kids and many others.

You can connect with Tes at:
tes@lincchurch.com
Instagram and Facebook @tesjahnig

Check out The Linc Sisterhood https://lincsisterhood.com/ @thelincsisterhood and **subscribe to The Linc Sisterhood Podcast** on YouTube, Apple podcasts and Spotify.

www.ingramcontent.com/pod-product-compliance
Lightning Source LLC
LaVergne TN
LVHW041542070426
835507LV00011B/875